Back to the sea

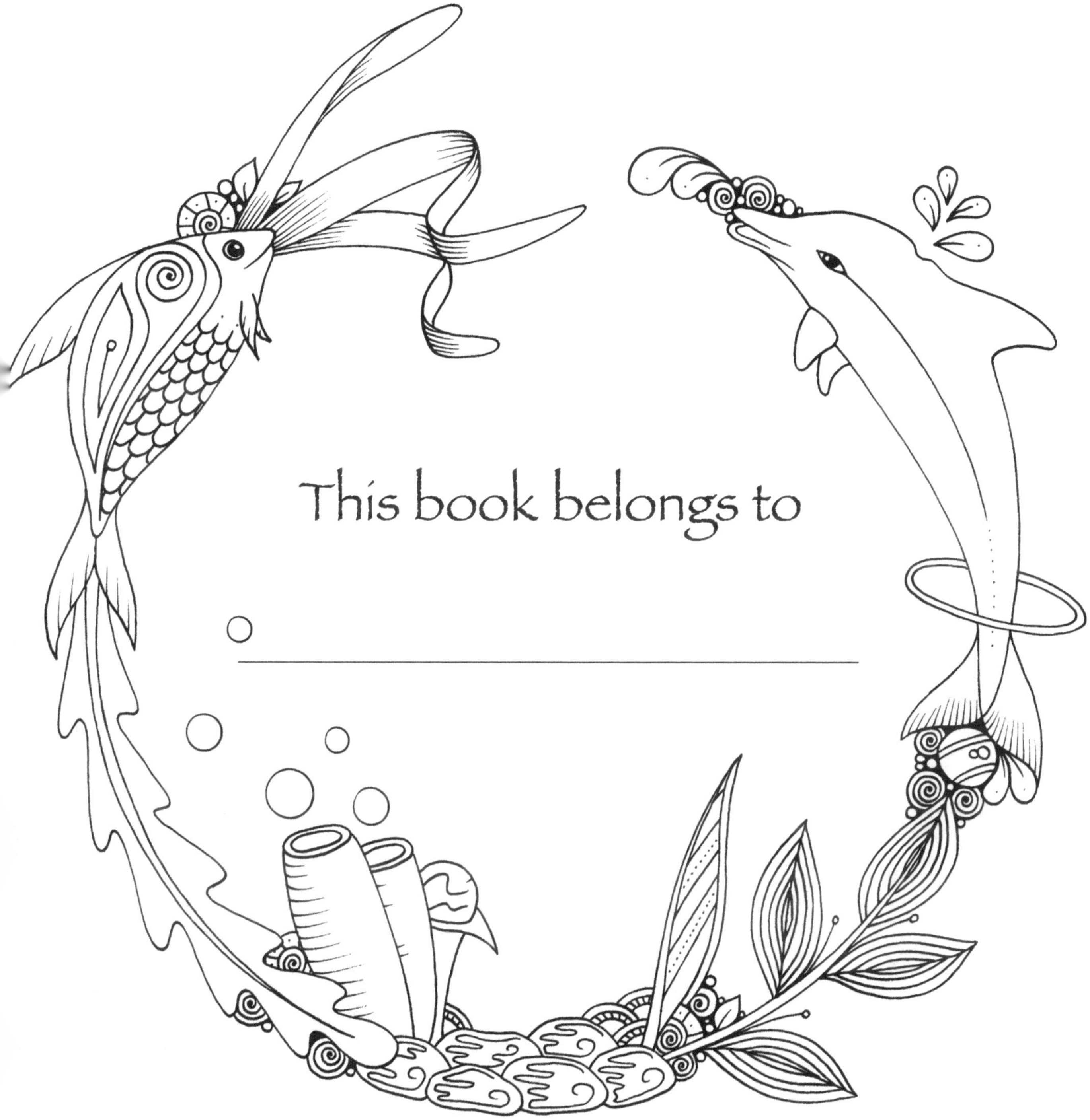

This book belongs to

____

Maud Feral-Chauveau

Maud Feral-Chauveau (MFC)

Back to the sea

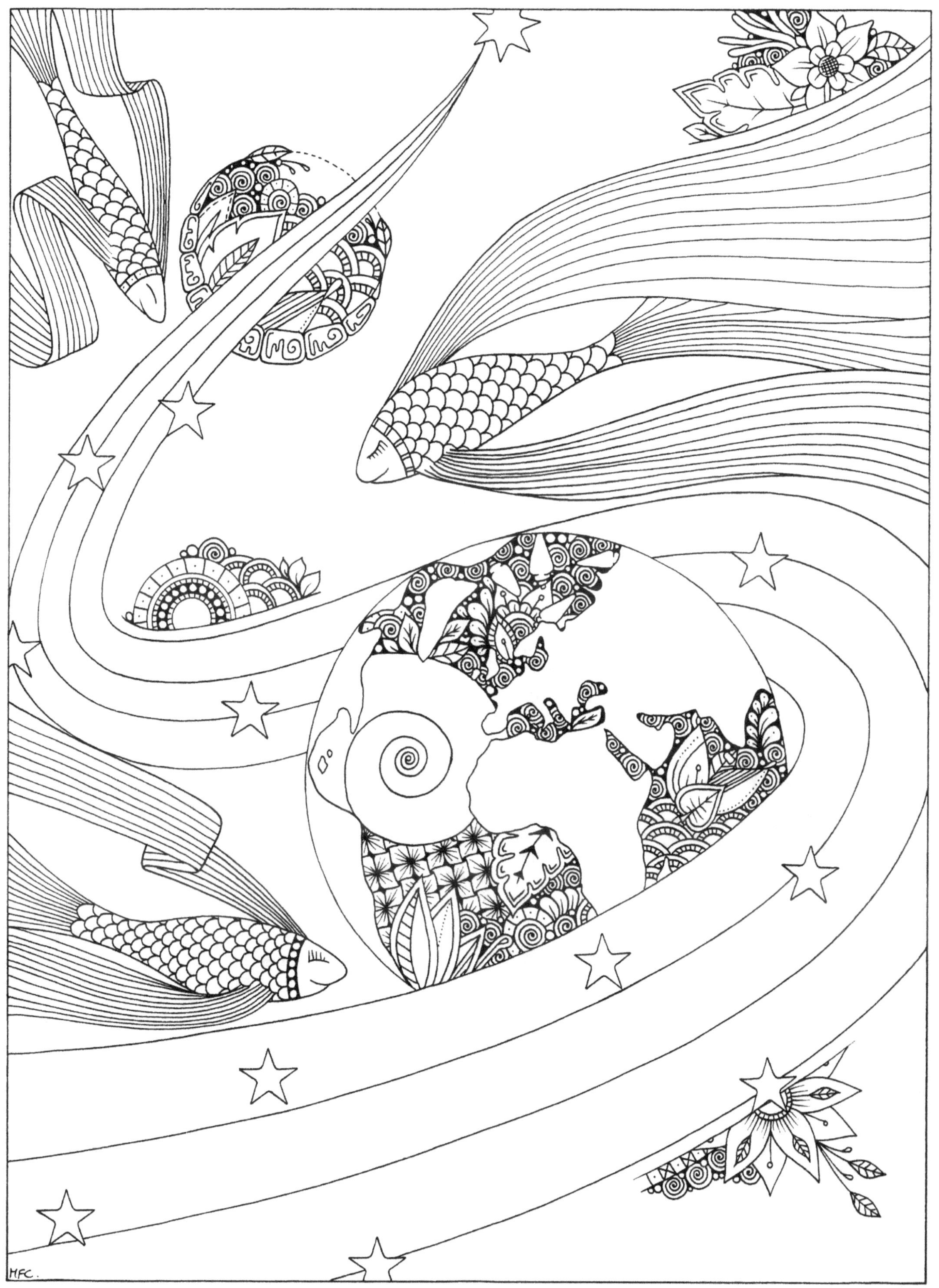

Maud Feral-Chauveau (MFC)

Back to the sea

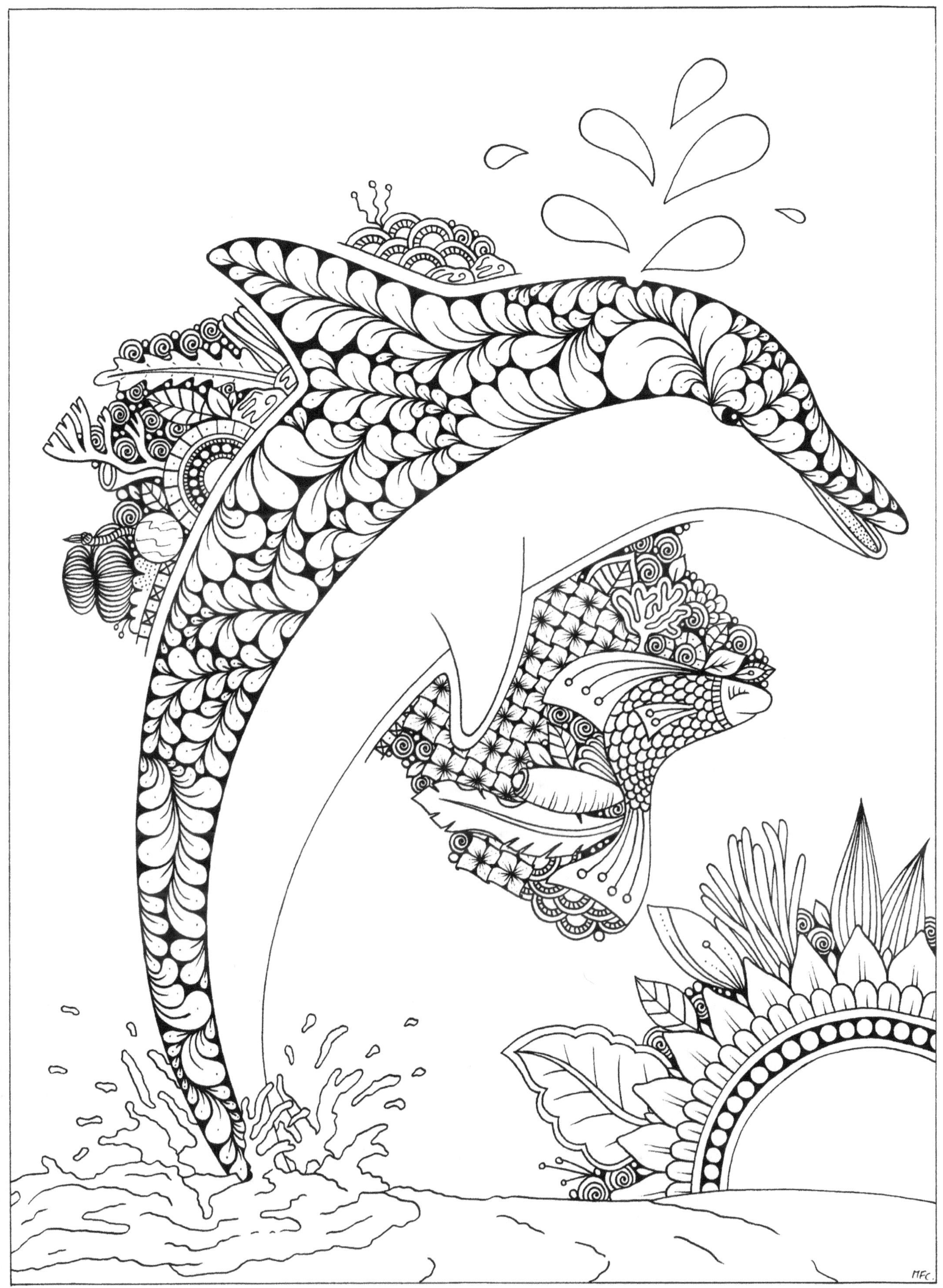

Maud Feral-Chauveau (MFC)

Back to the sea

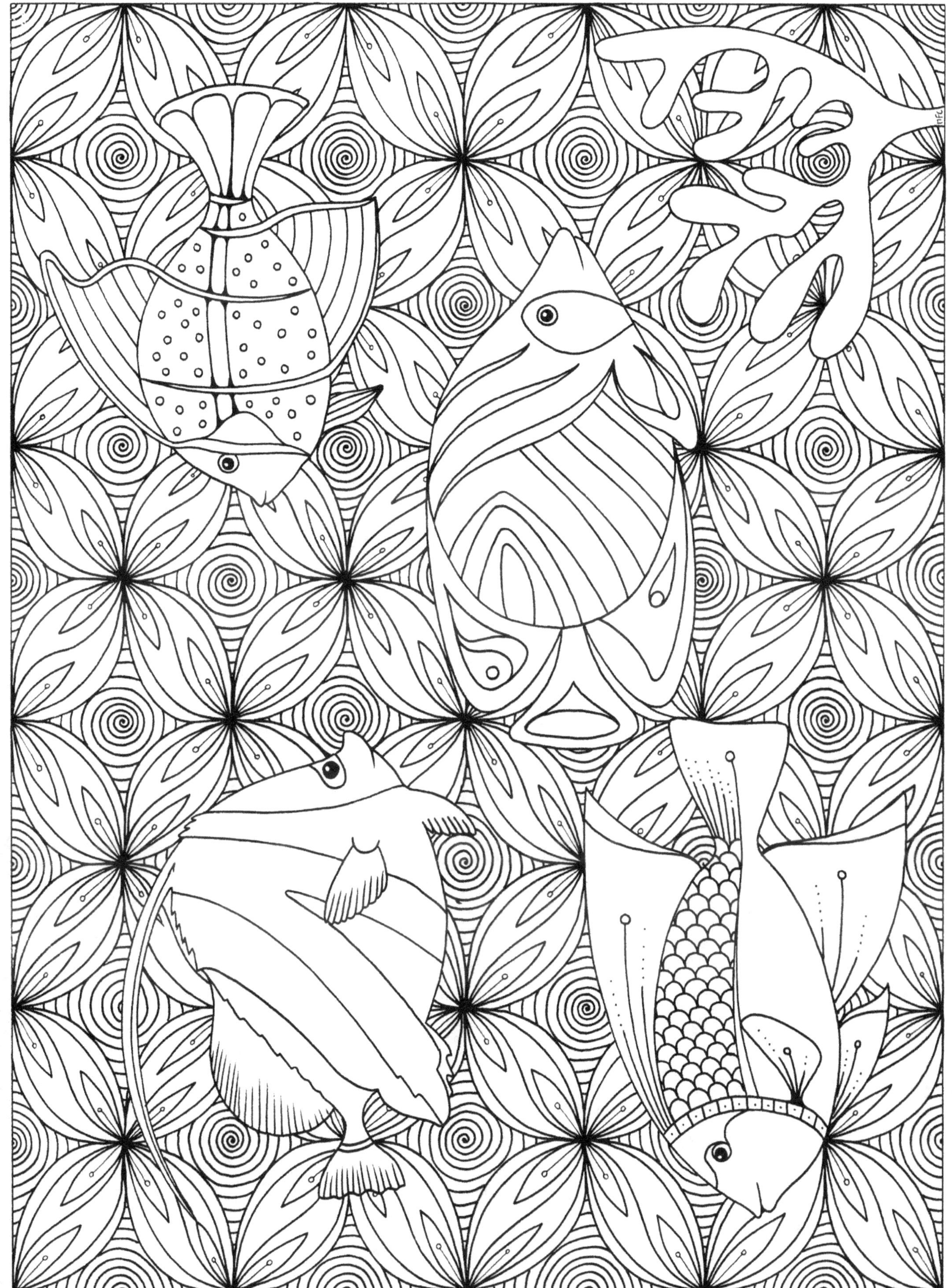

Maud Feral-Chauveau (MFC)

Back to the sea

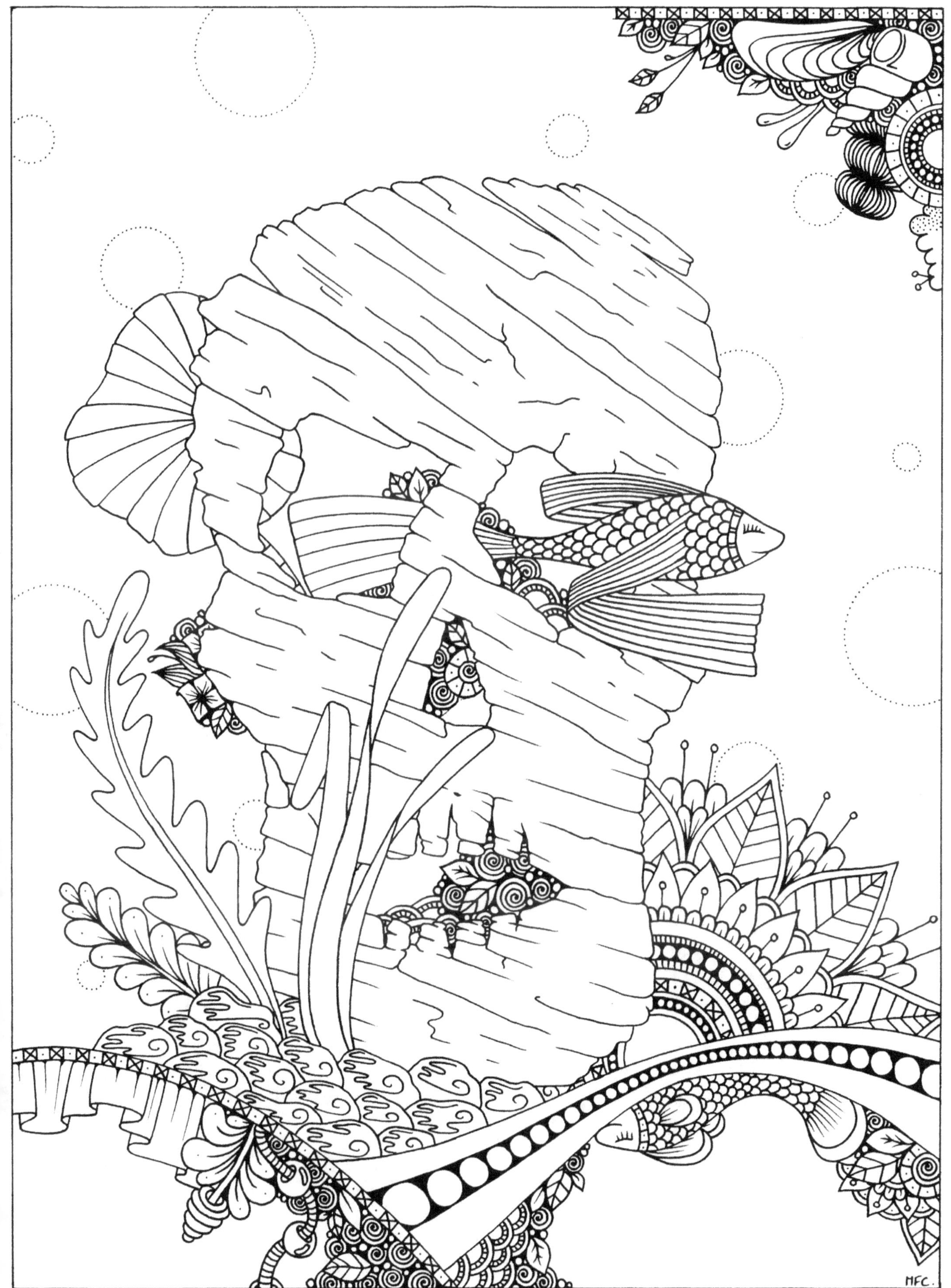

Maud Feral-Chauveau (MFC)

Back to the sea

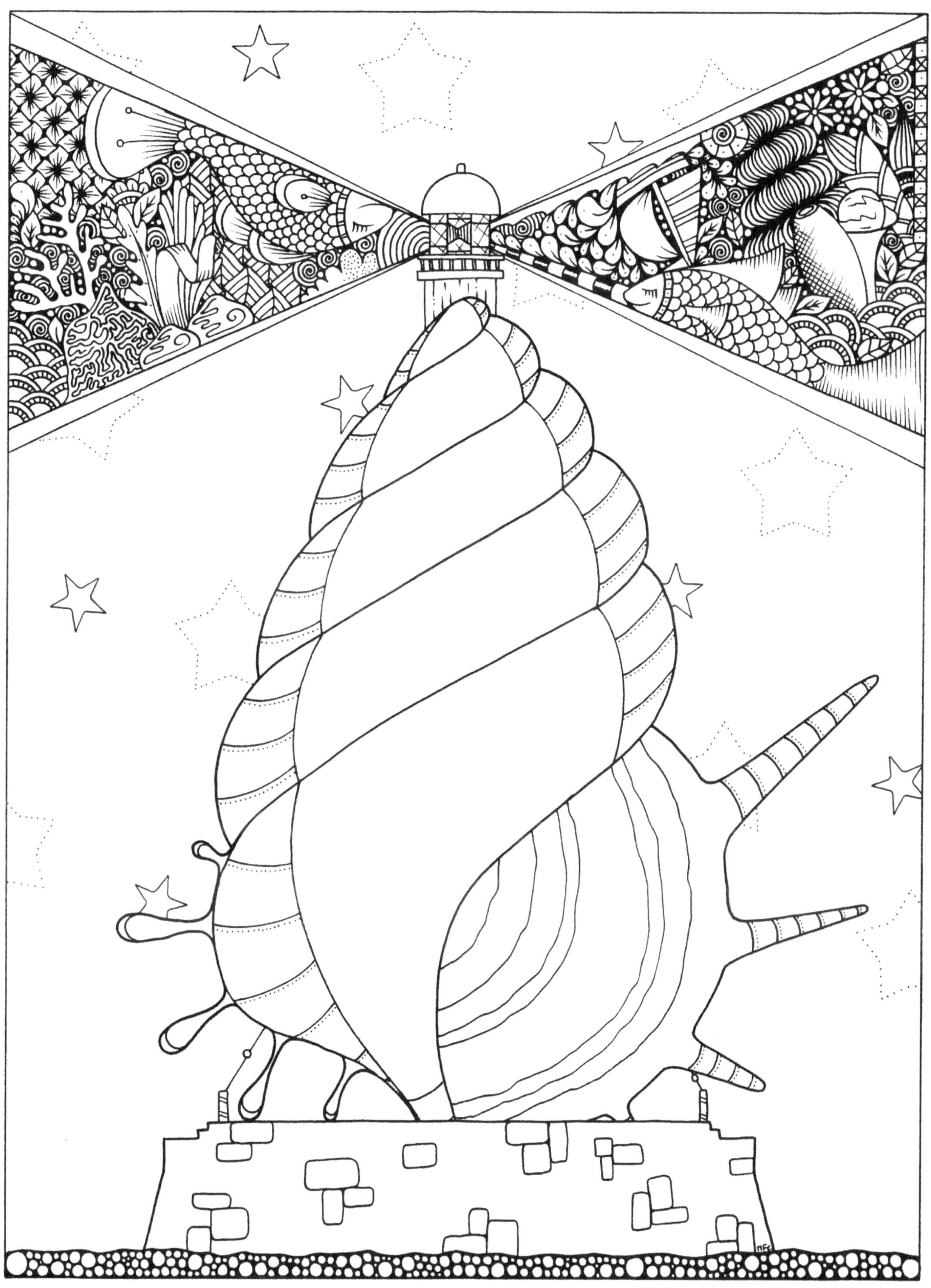

Maud Feral-Chauveau (MFC)

Back to the sea

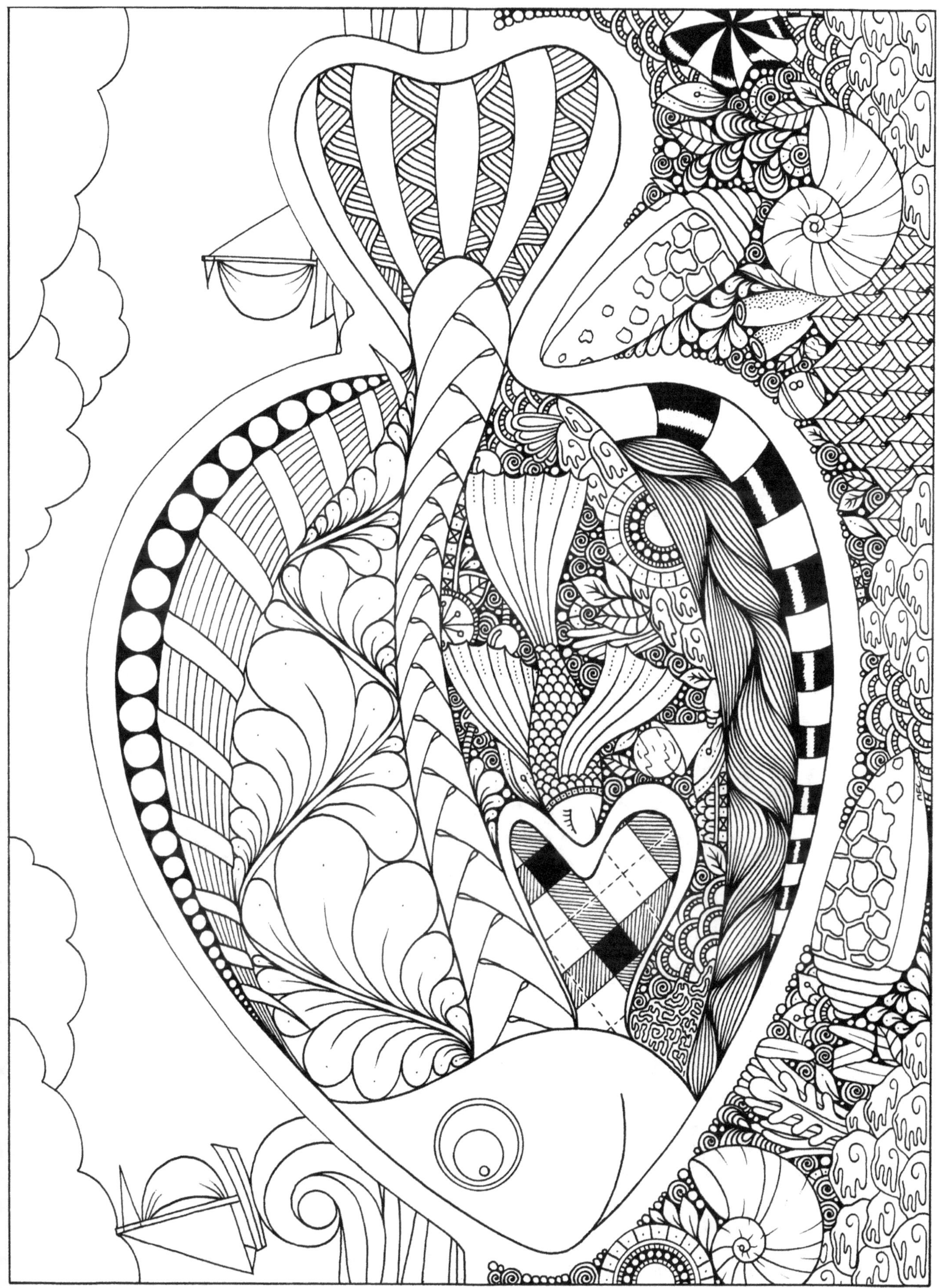

Maud Feral-Chauveau (MFC)

Back to the sea

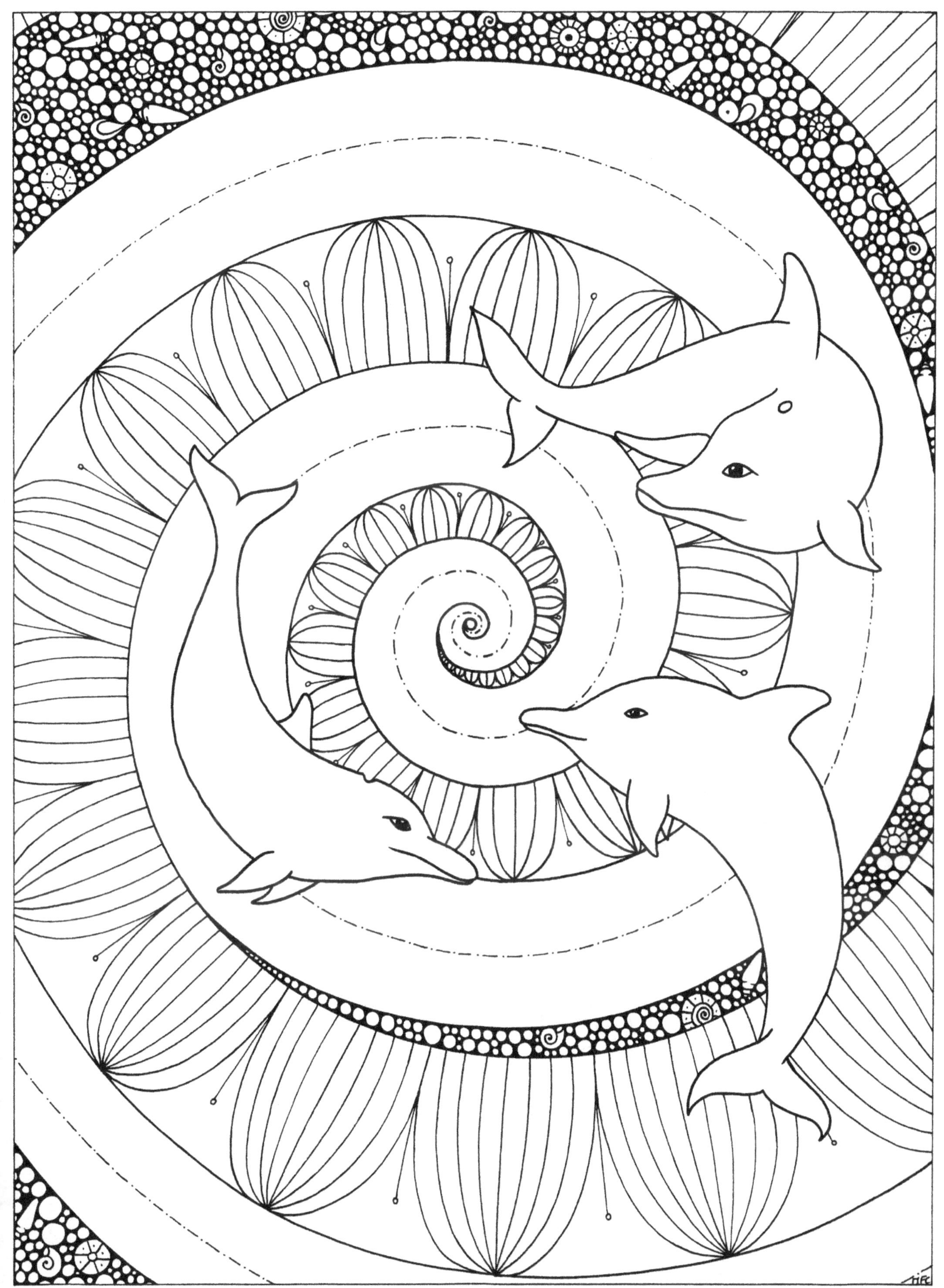

Maud Feral-Chauveau (MFC)

Back to the sea

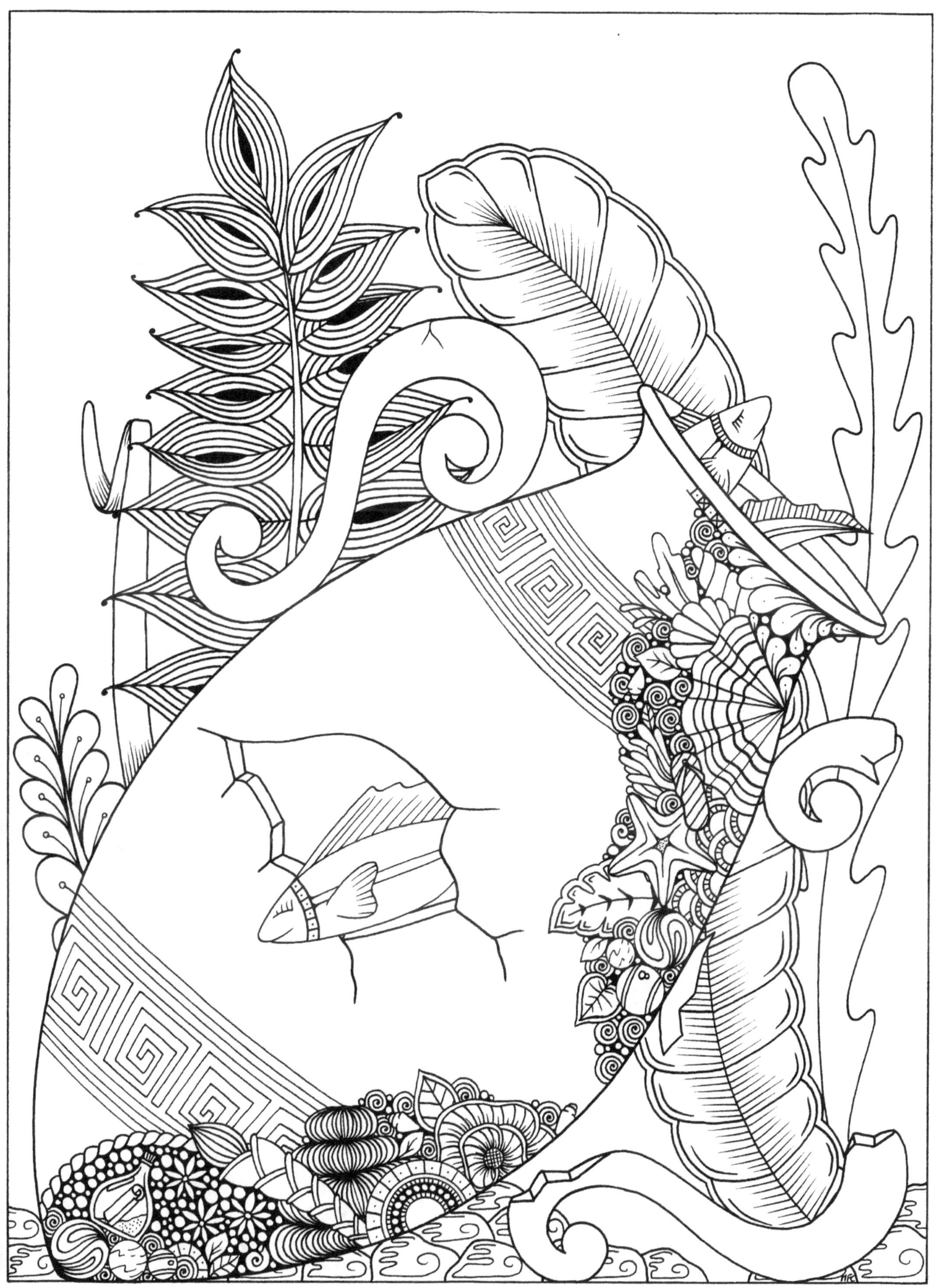

Maud Feral-Chauveau (MFC)

Back to the sea

Maud Feral-Chauveau (MFC)

Back to the sea

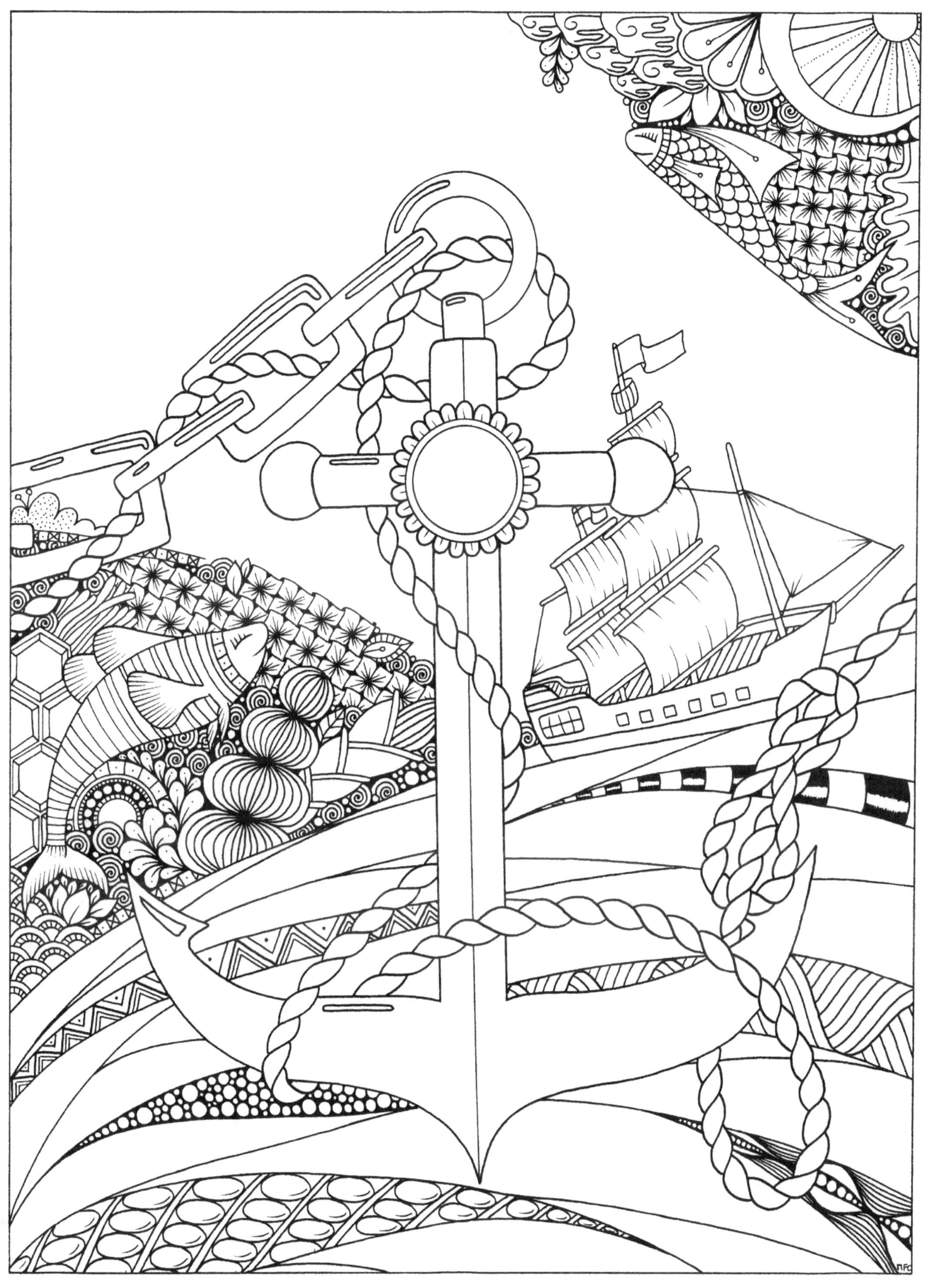

Maud Feral-Chauveau (MFC)

Back to the sea

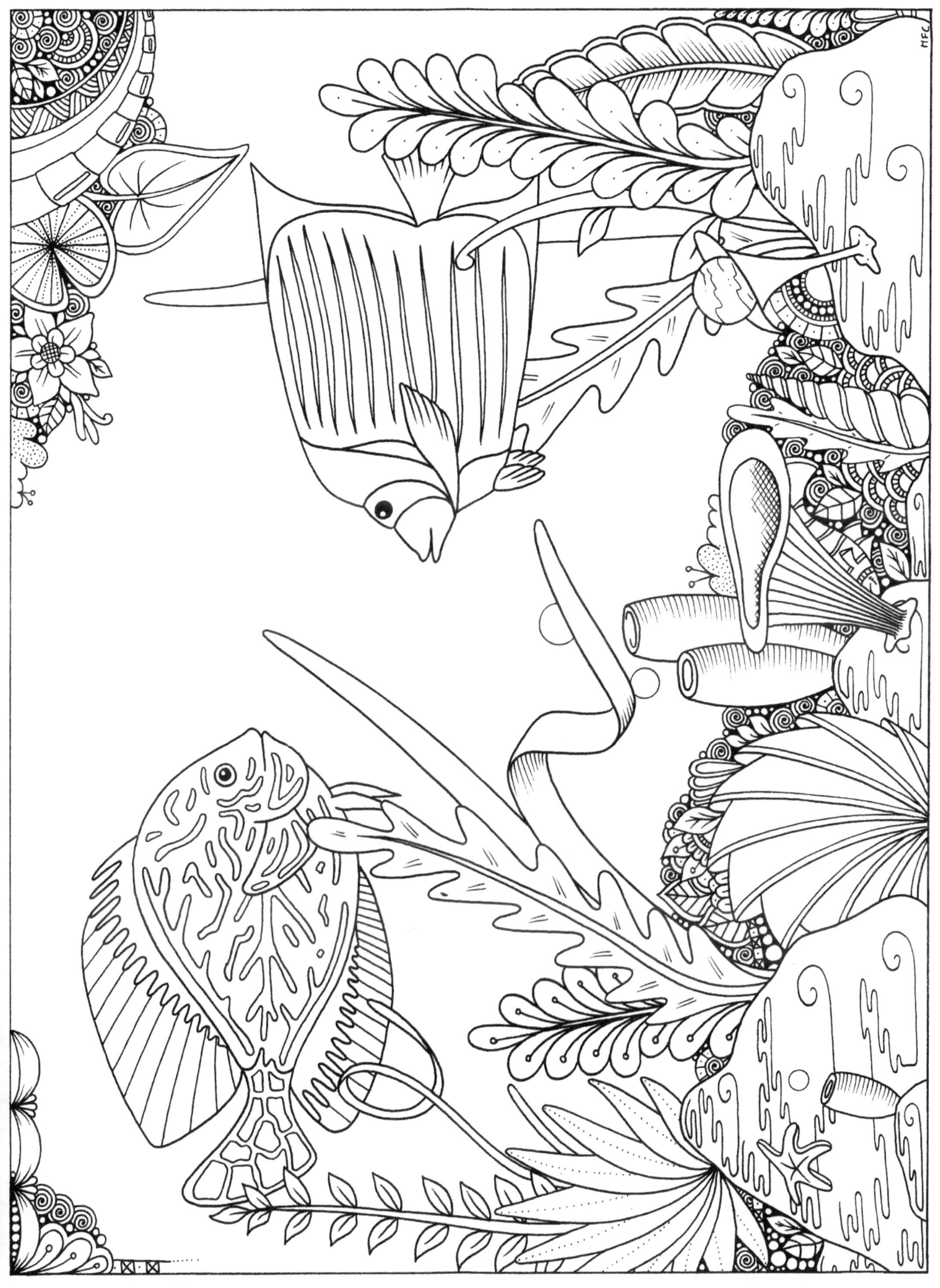

Maud Feral-Chauveau (MFC)

Back to the sea

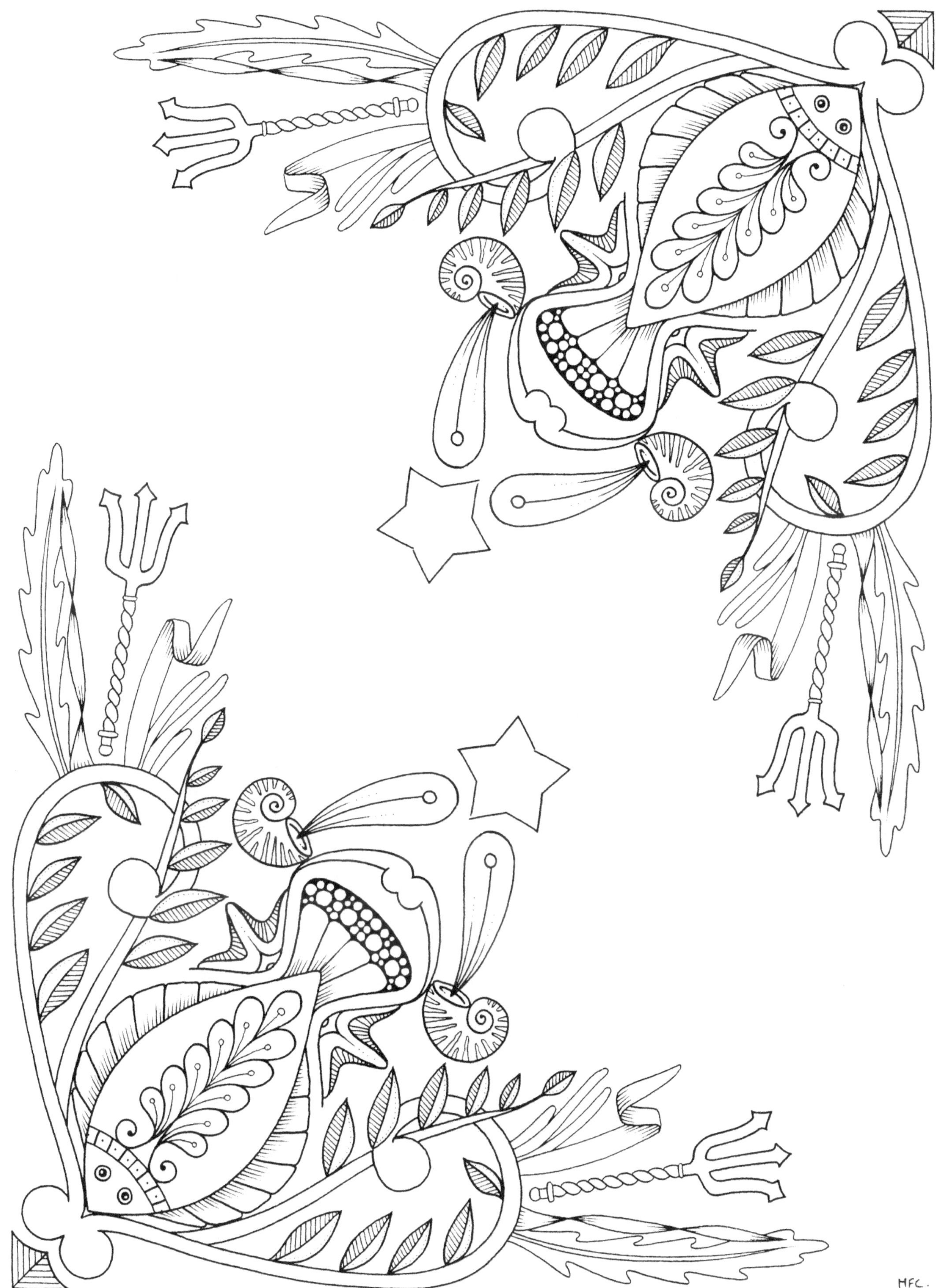

Maud Feral-Chauveau (MFC)

Back to the sea

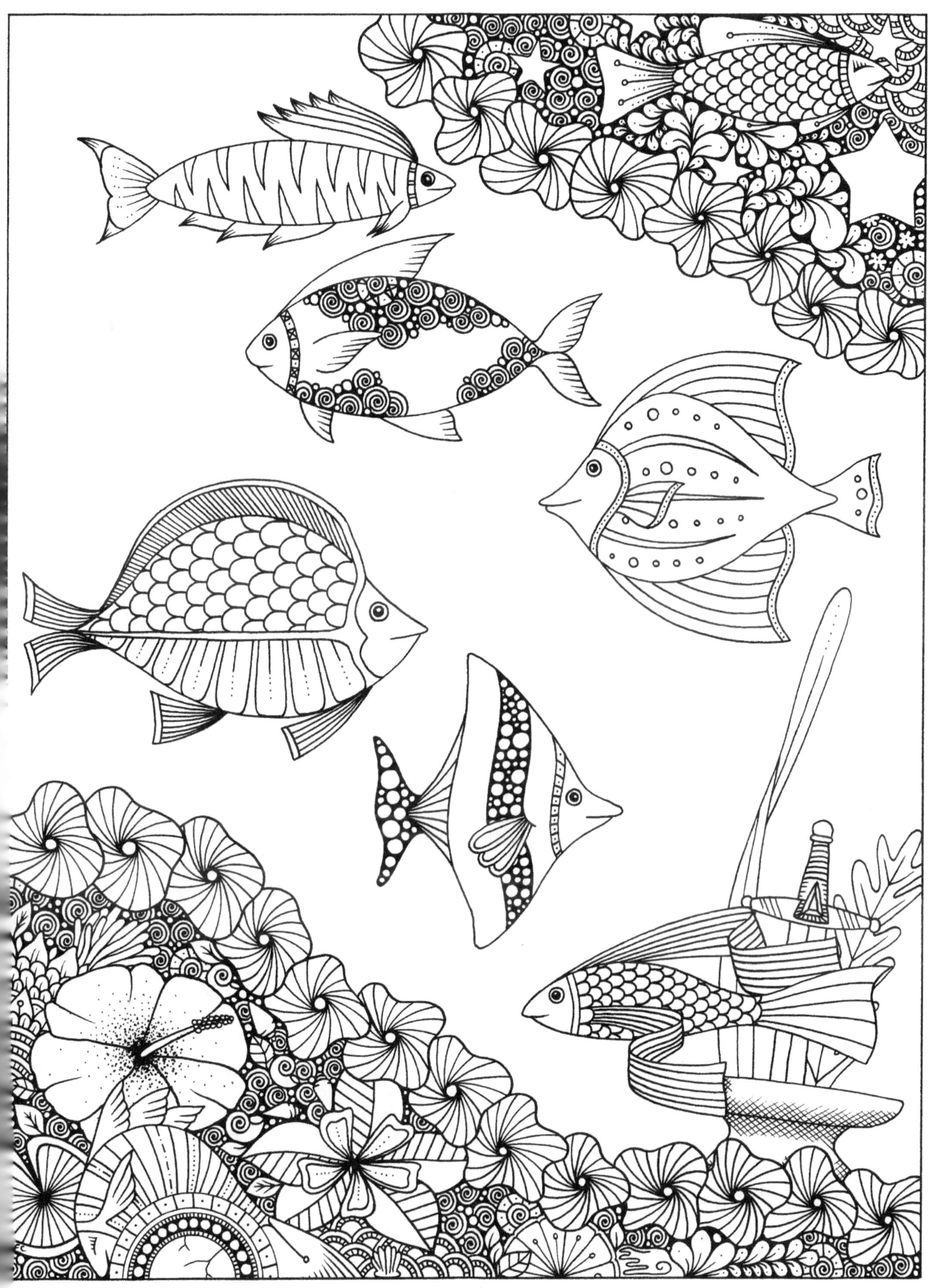

Maud Feral-Chauveau (MFC)

Back to the sea

Maud Feral-Chauveau (MFC)

Back to the sea

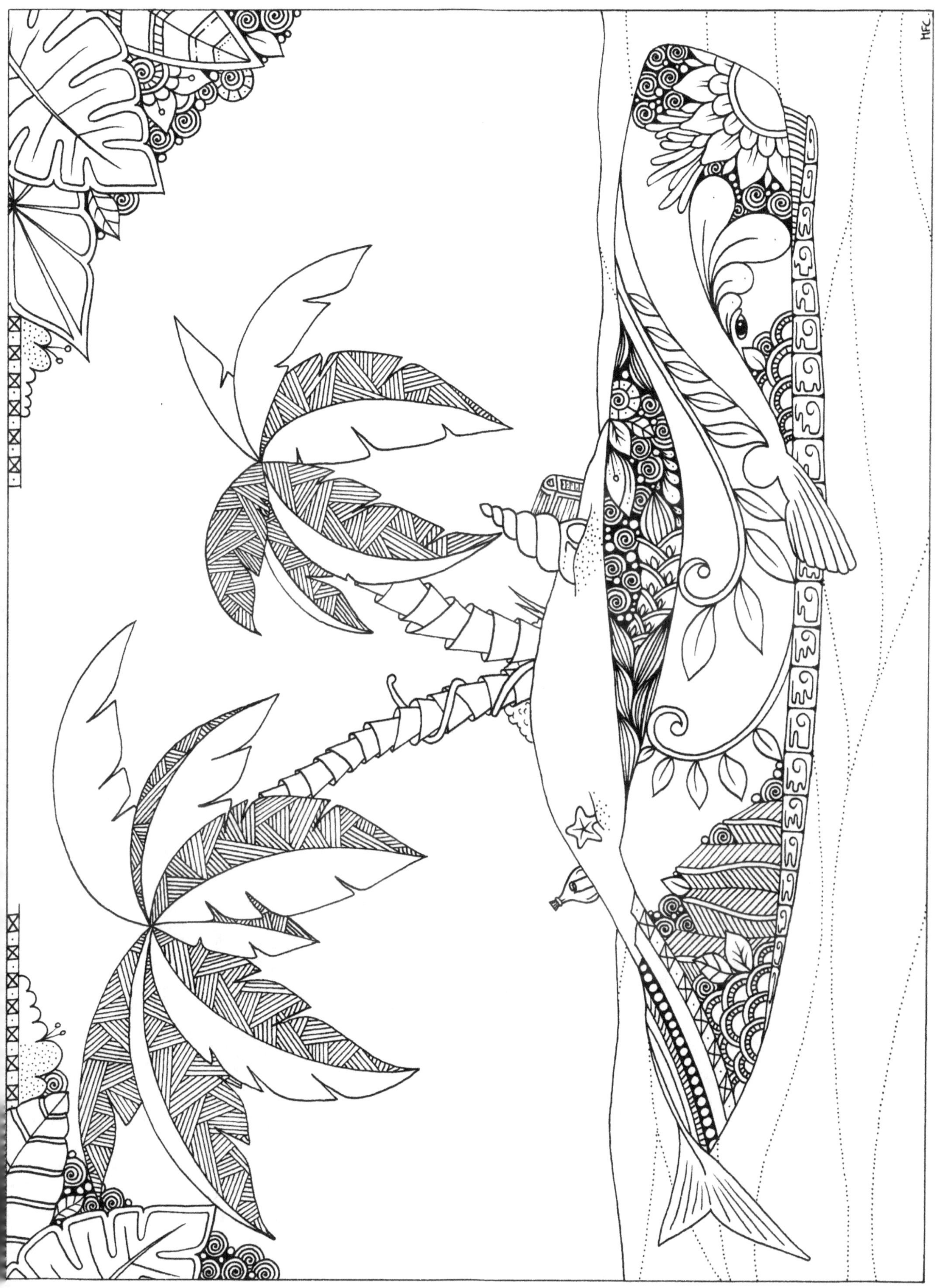

Maud Feral-Chauveau (MFC)

Back to the sea

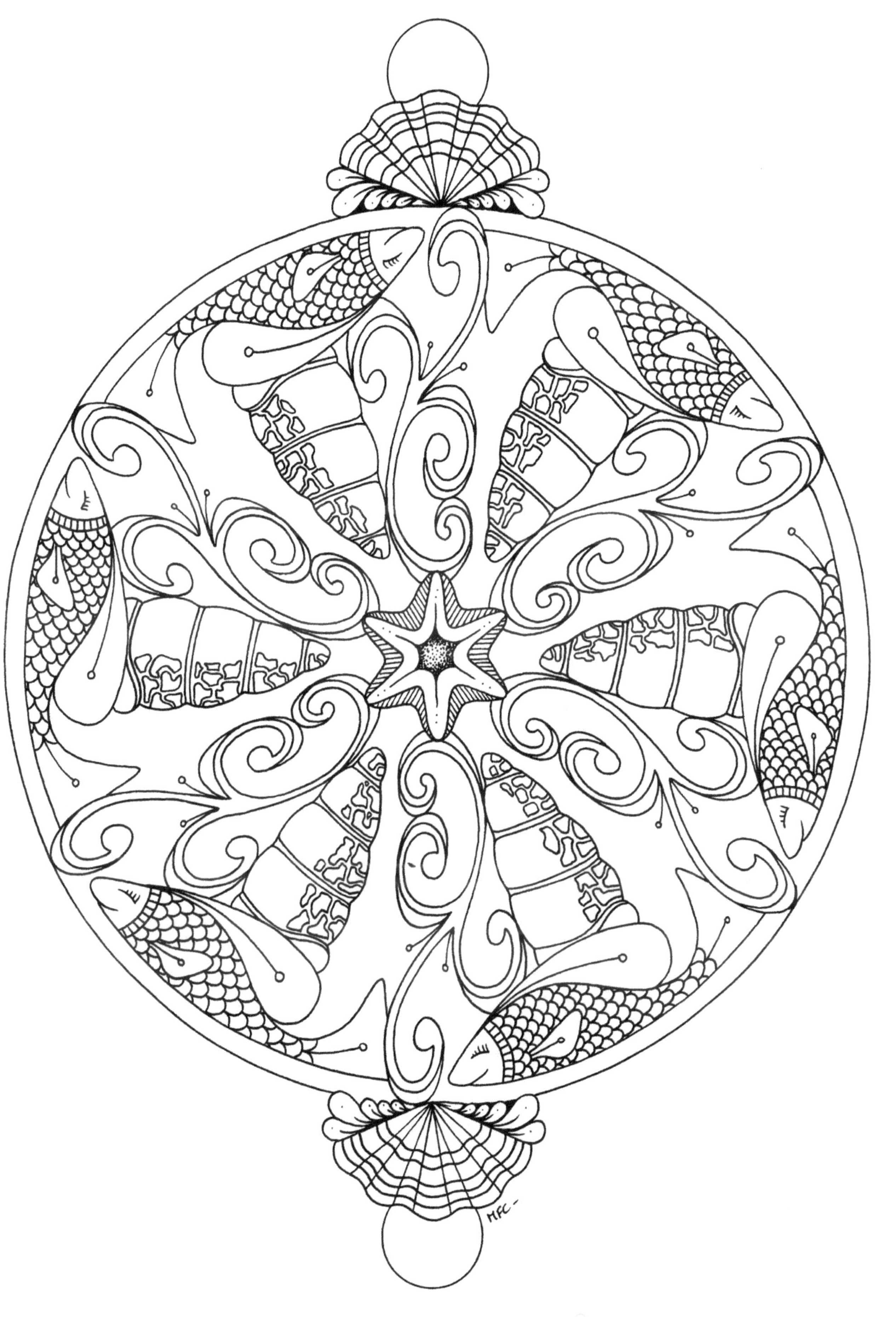

Maud Feral-Chauveau (MFC)

Back to the sea

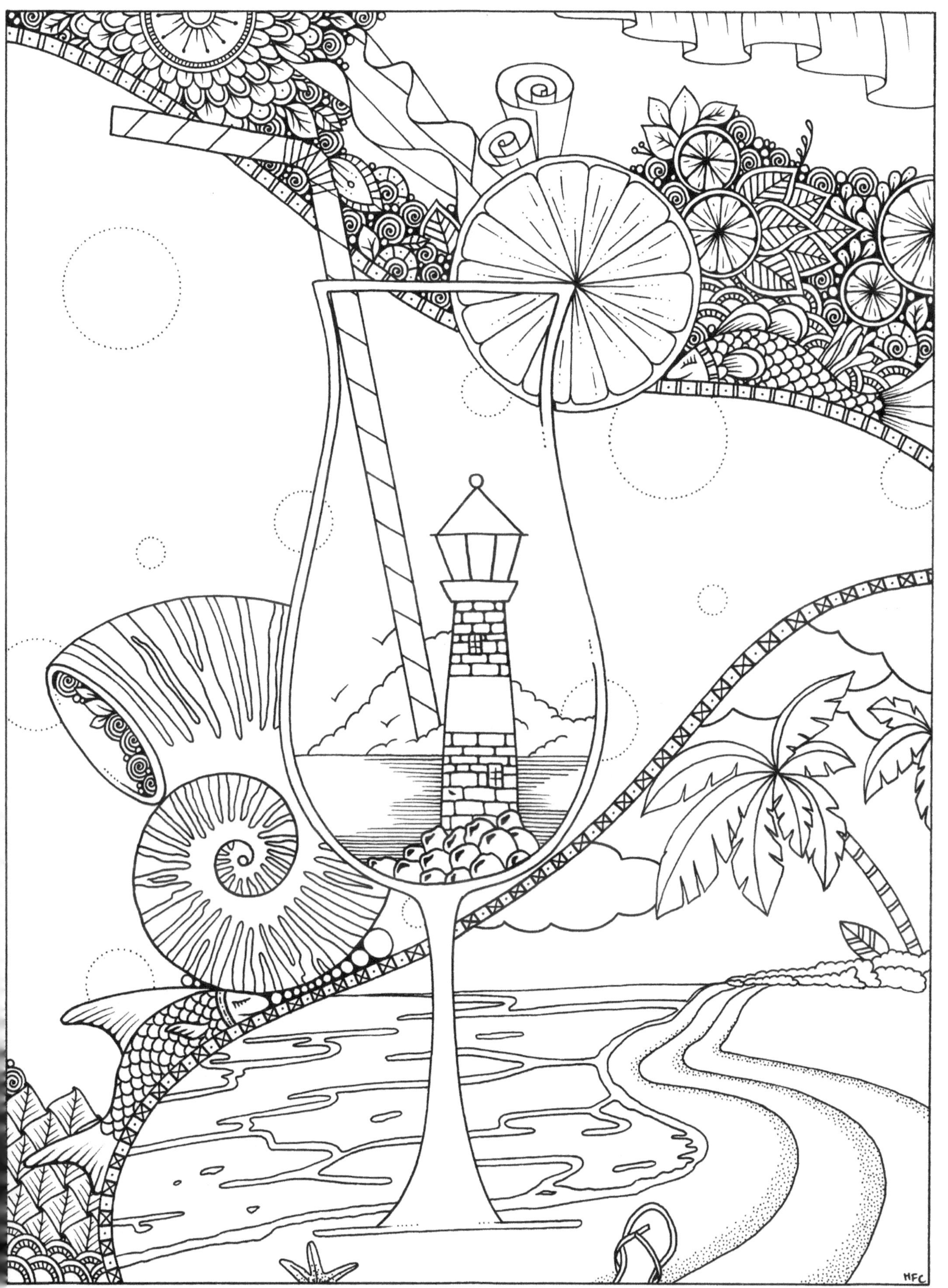

Maud Feral-Chauveau (MFC)

Back to the sea

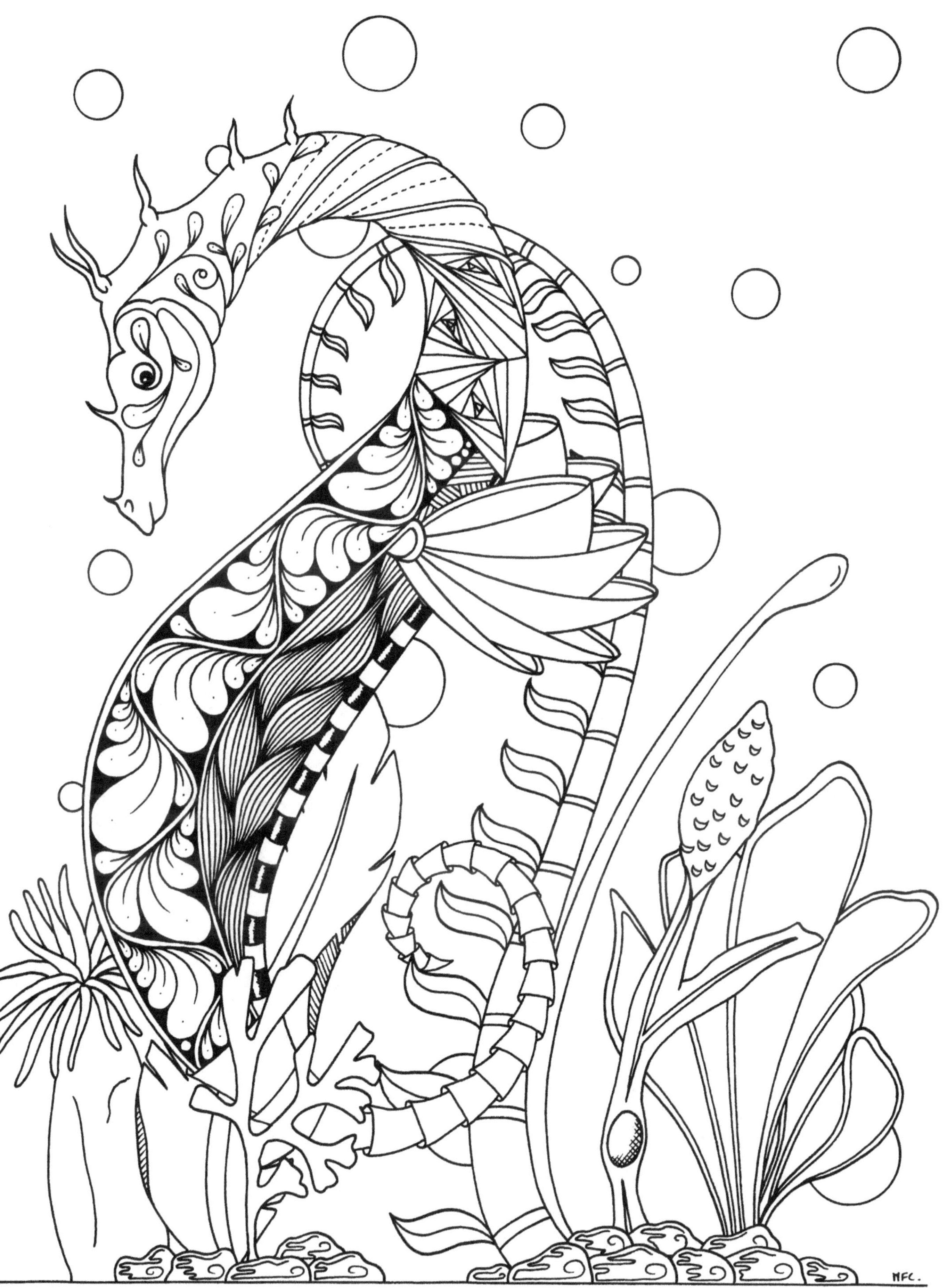

Maud Feral-Chauveau (MFC)

Back to the sea

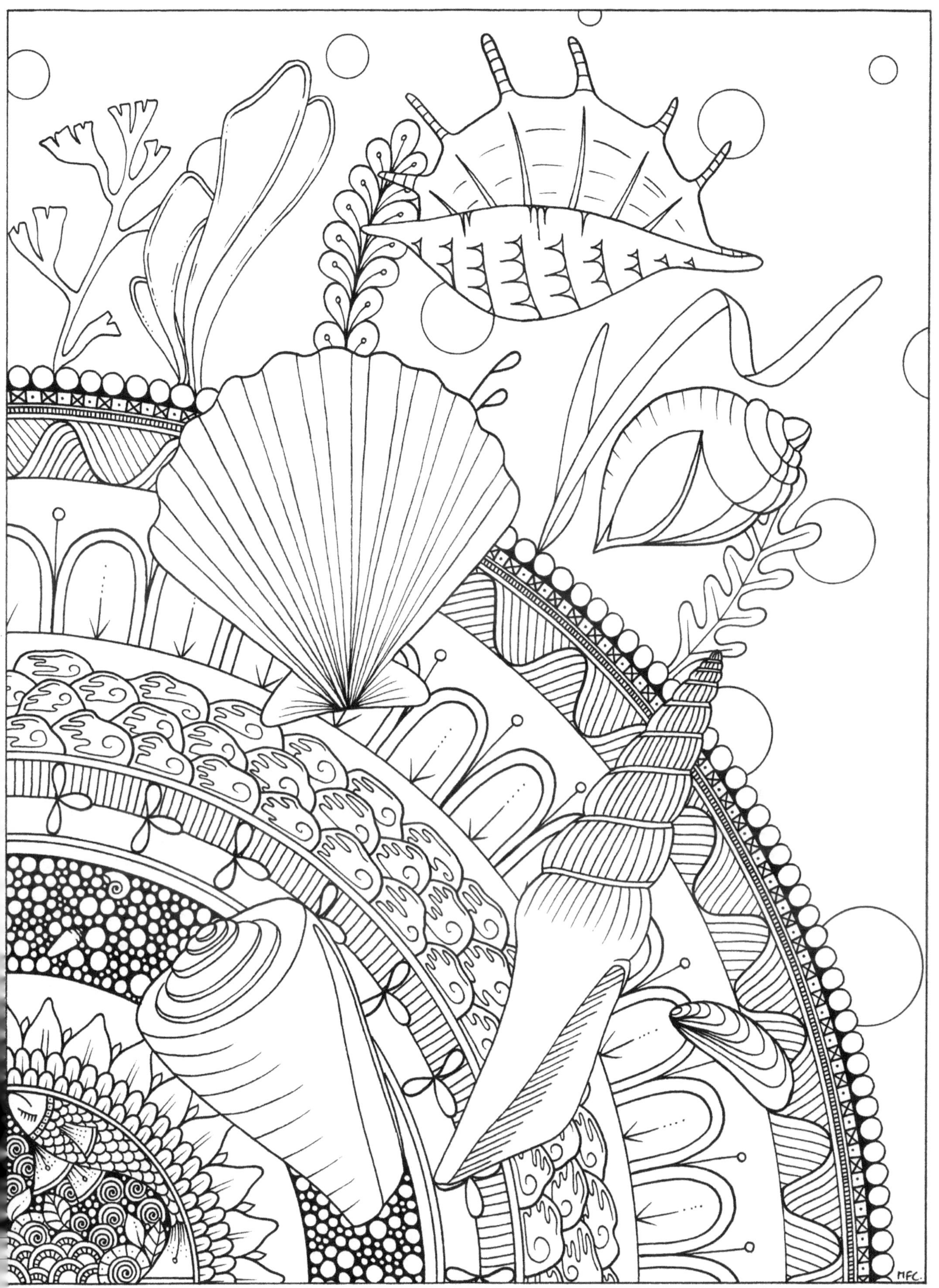

Maud Feral-Chauveau (MFC)

Back to the sea

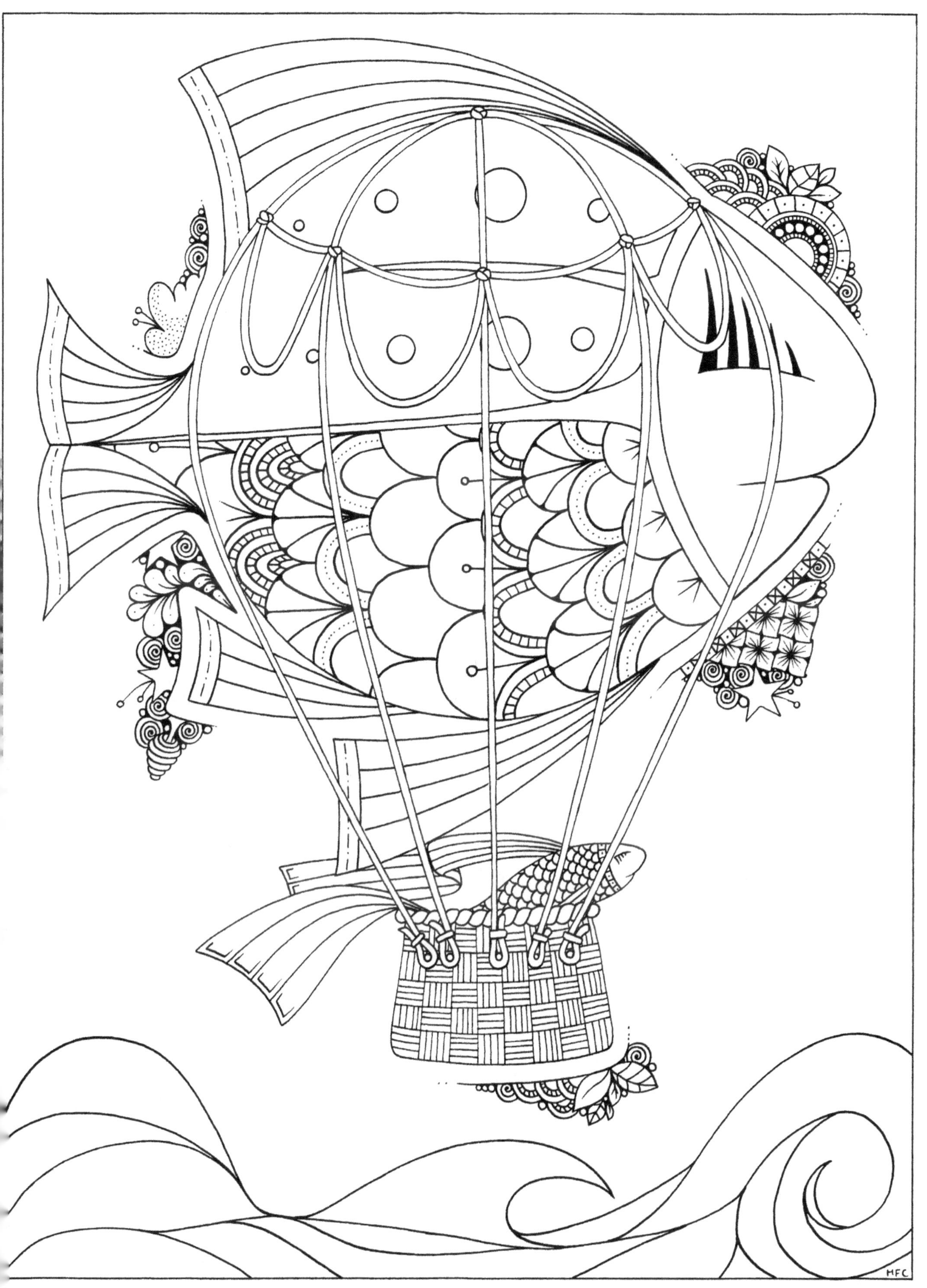

Maud Feral-Chauveau (MFC)

Back to the sea

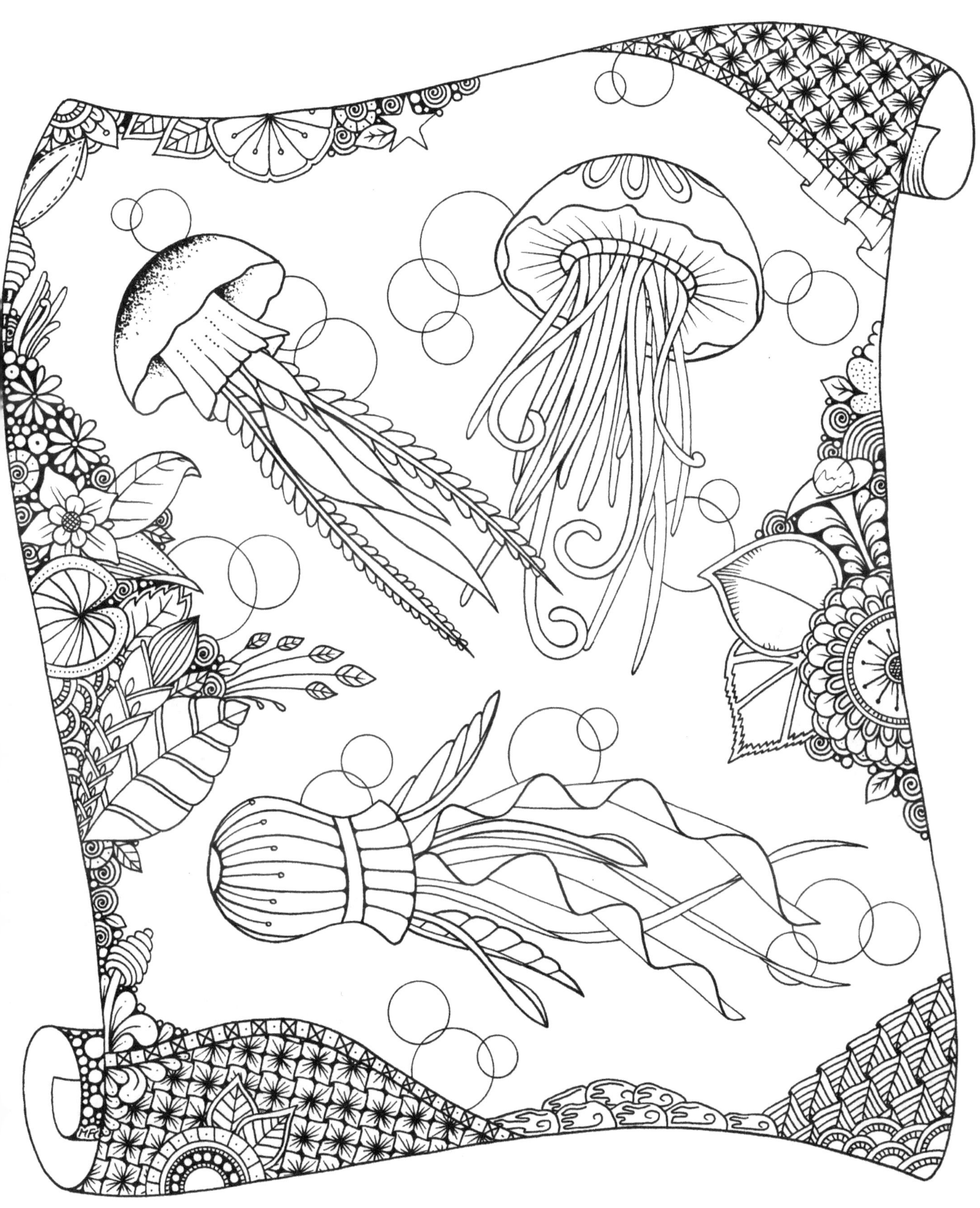

Maud Feral-Chauveau (MFC)

Back to the sea

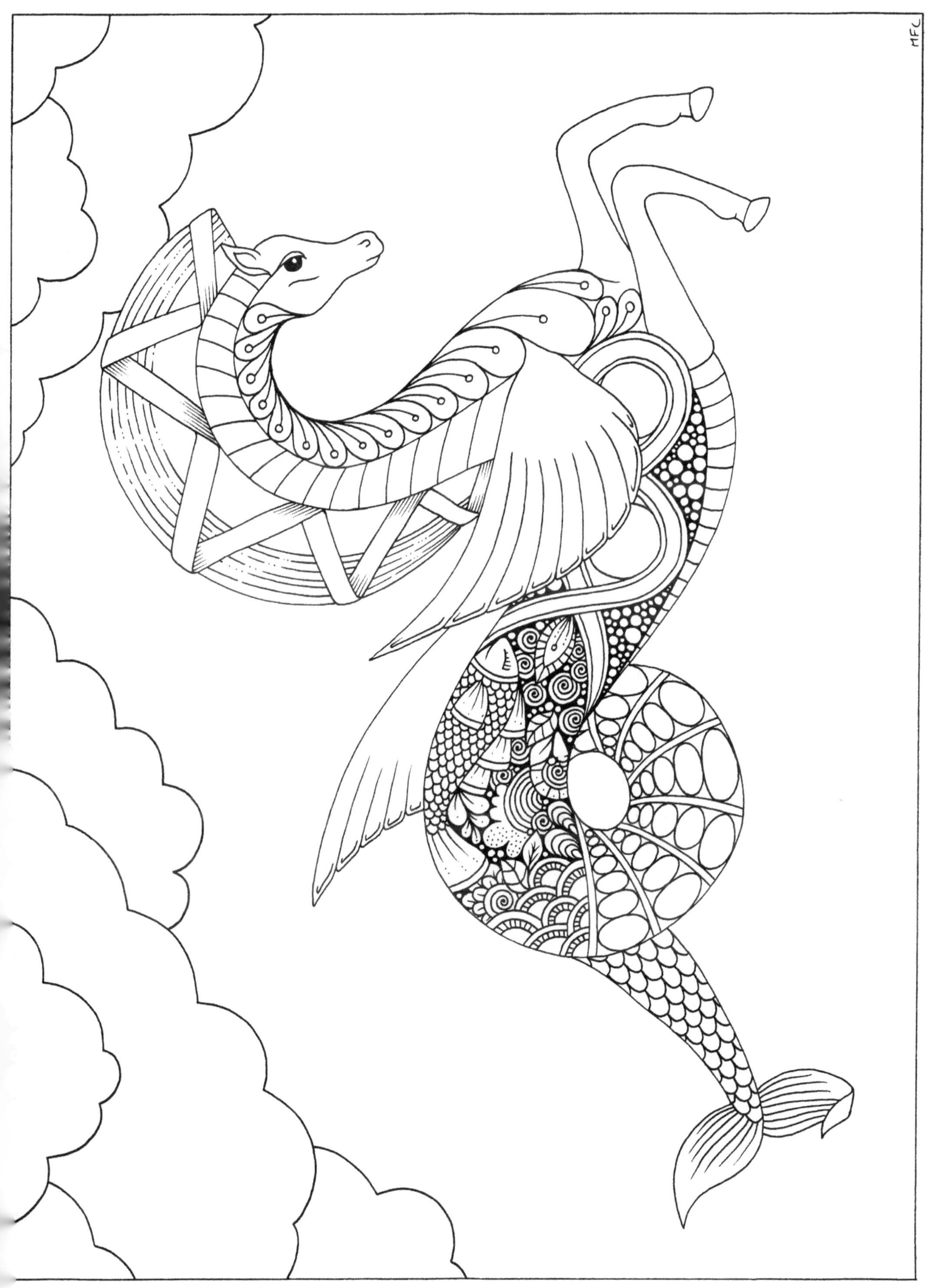
MFC

Maud Feral-Chauveau (MFC)

Back to the sea

Maud Feral-Chauveau (MFC)

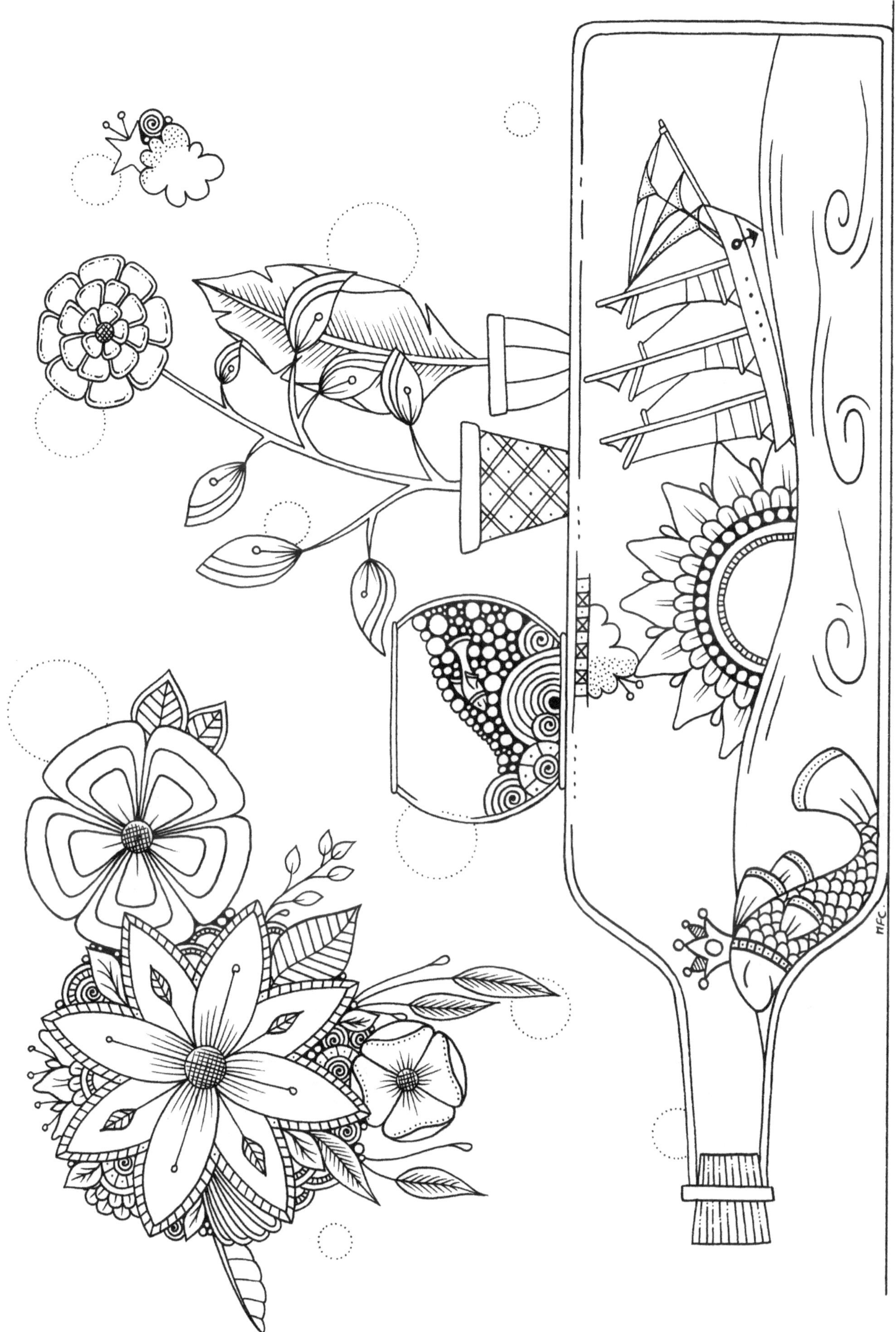

Maud Feral-Chauveau (MFC)

Back to the sea

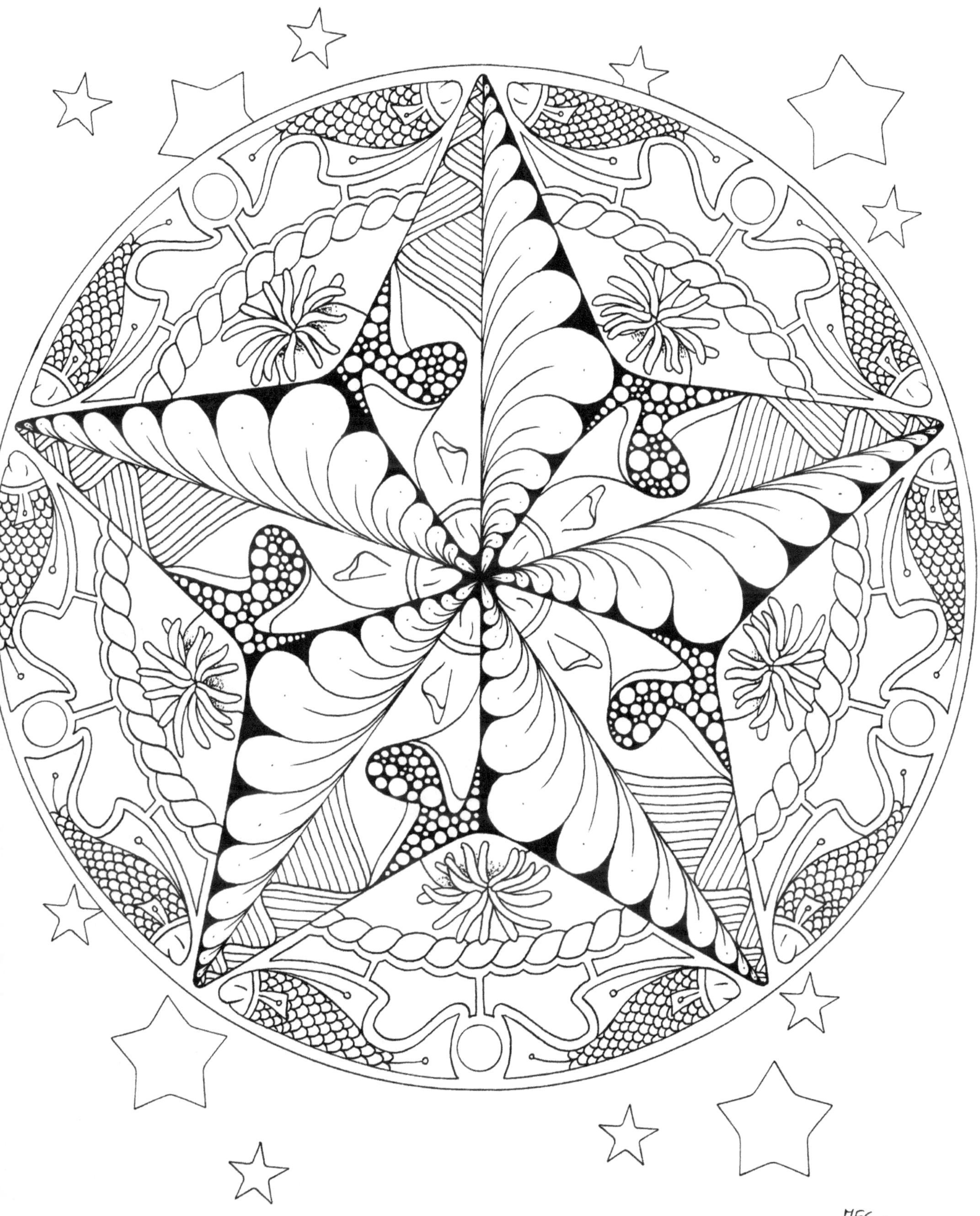

Maud Feral-Chauveau (MFC)

Back to the sea

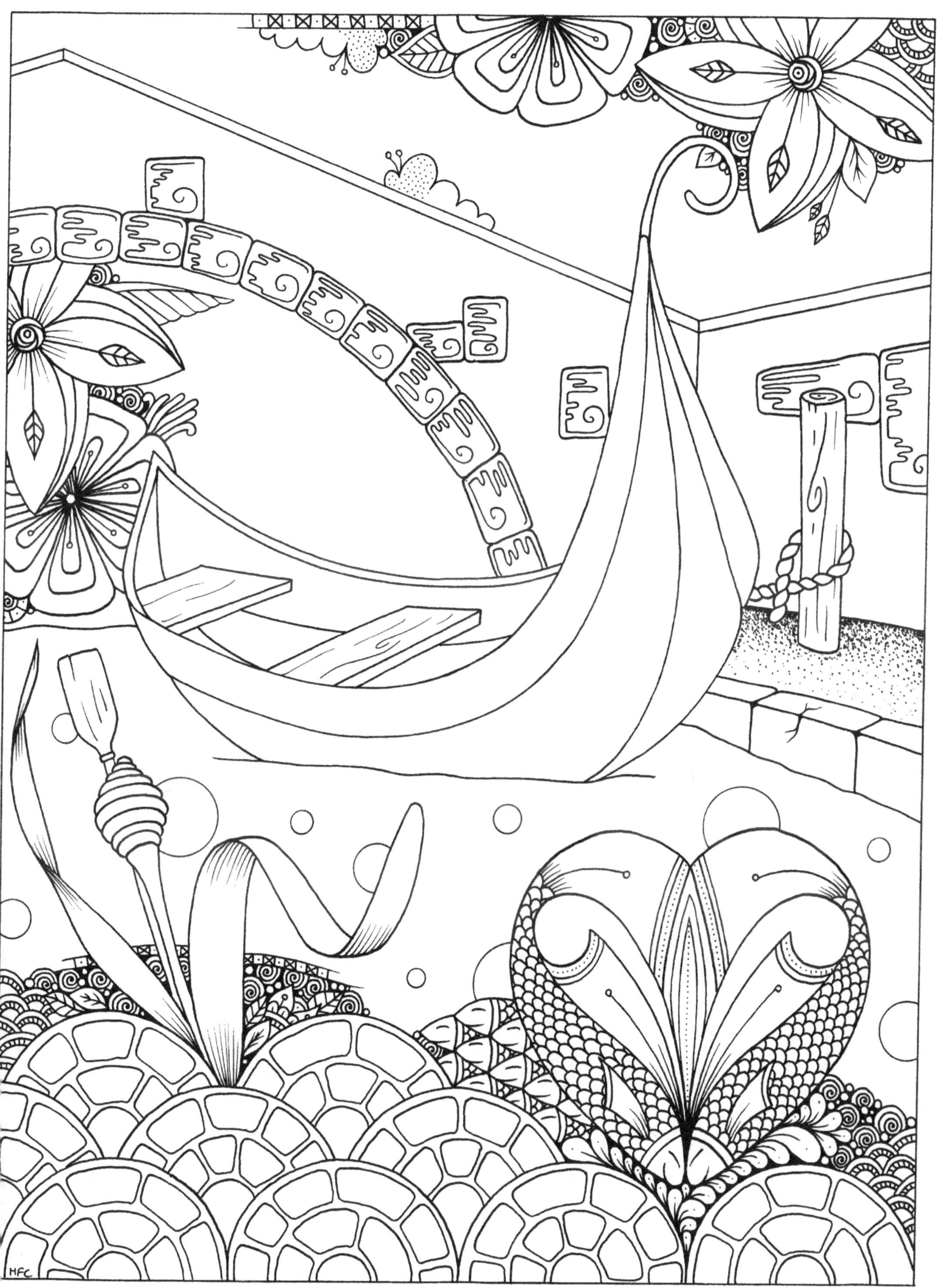

Maud Feral-Chauveau (MFC)

Back to the sea

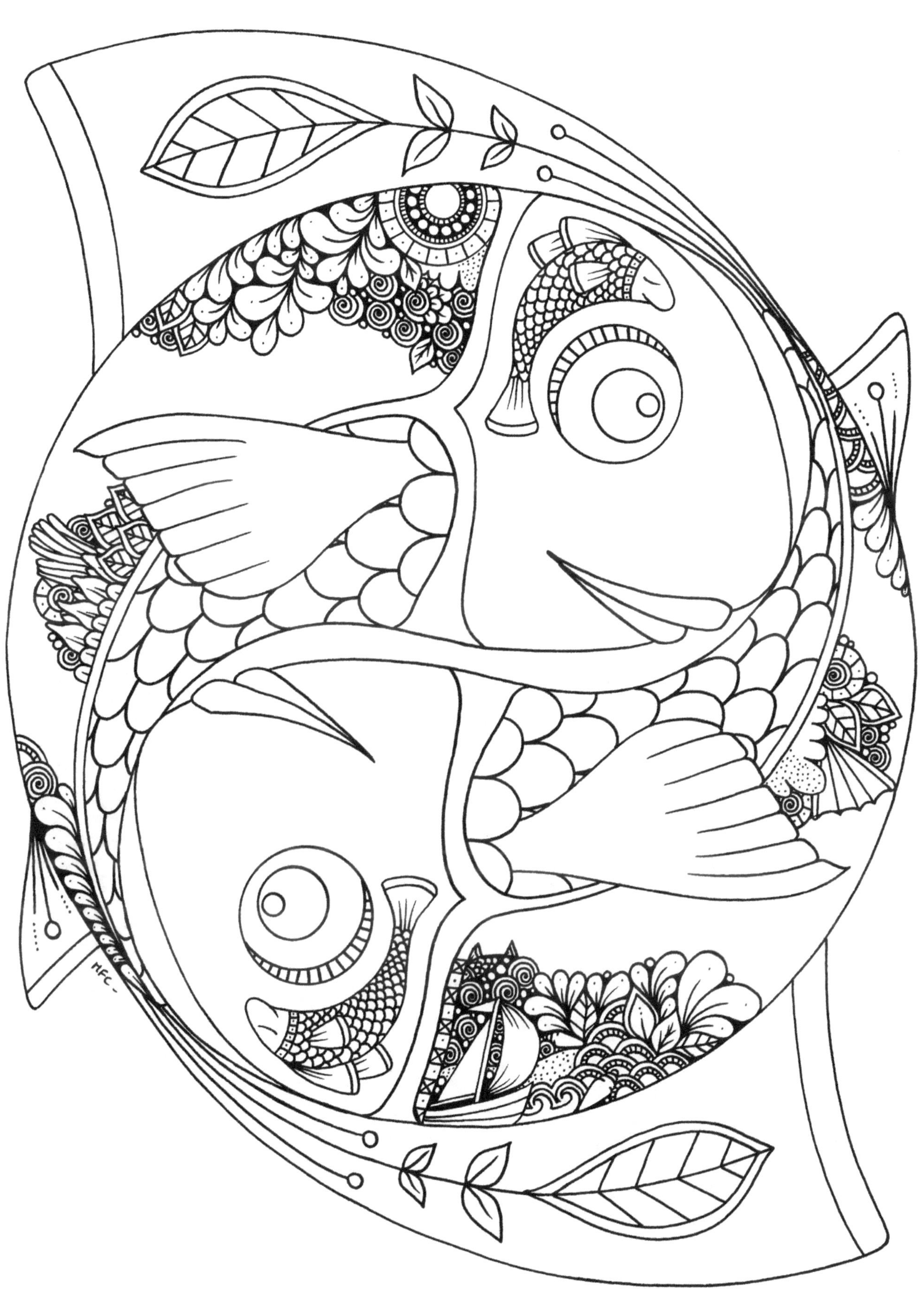

Maud Feral-Chauveau (MFC)

Back to the sea

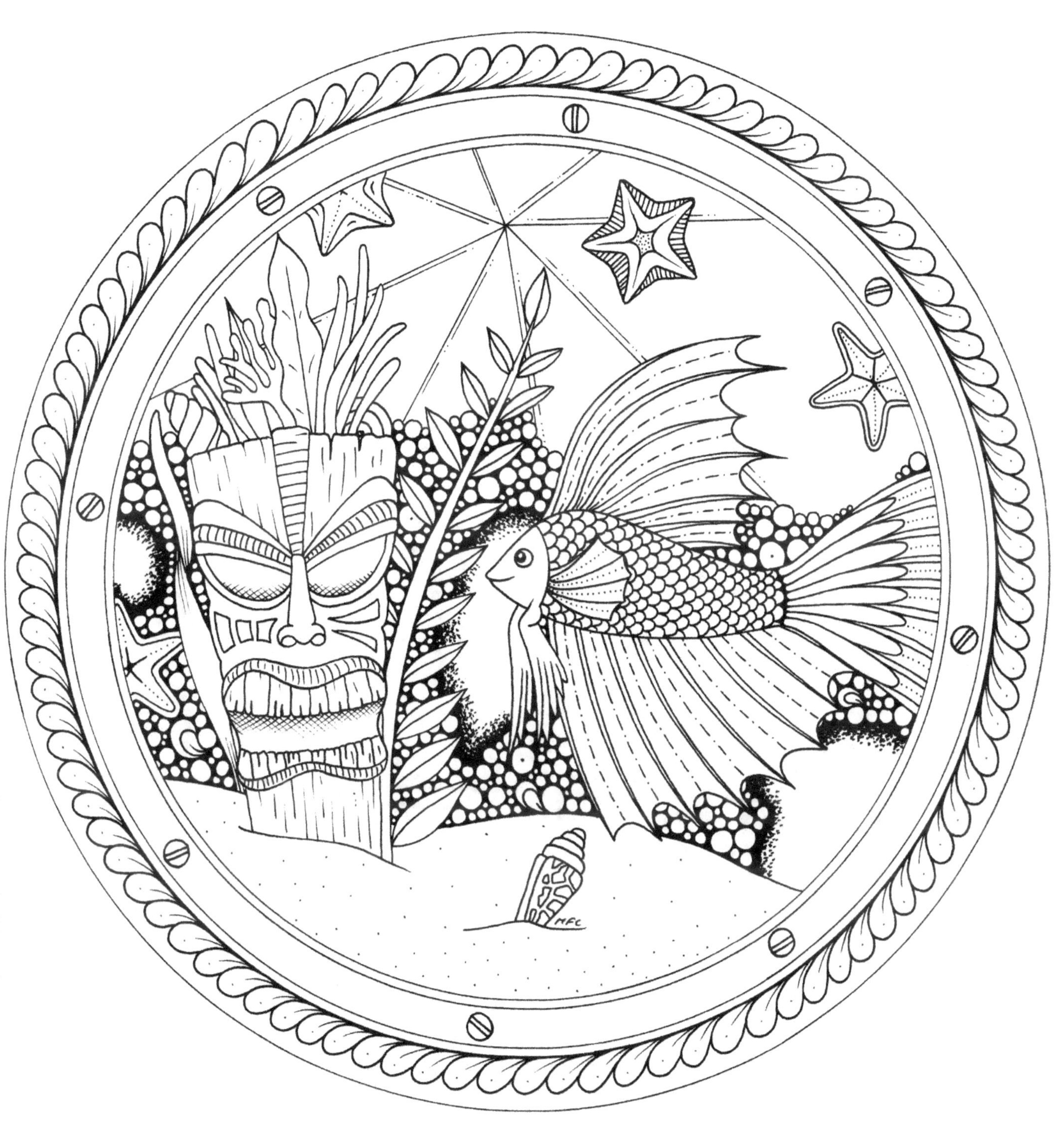

Maud Feral-Chauveau (MFC)

Back to the sea

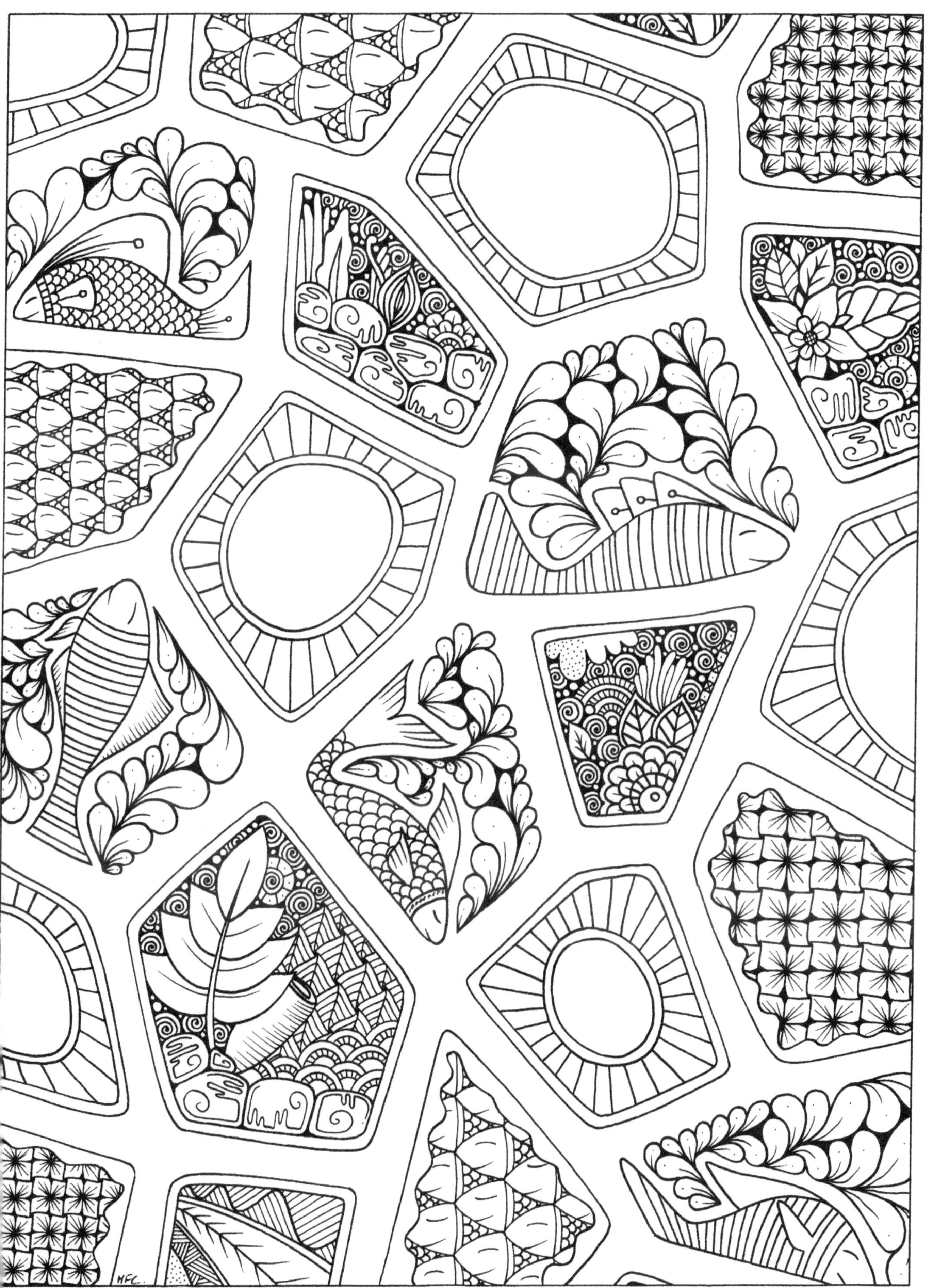

Maud Feral-Chauveau (MFC)

Back to the sea

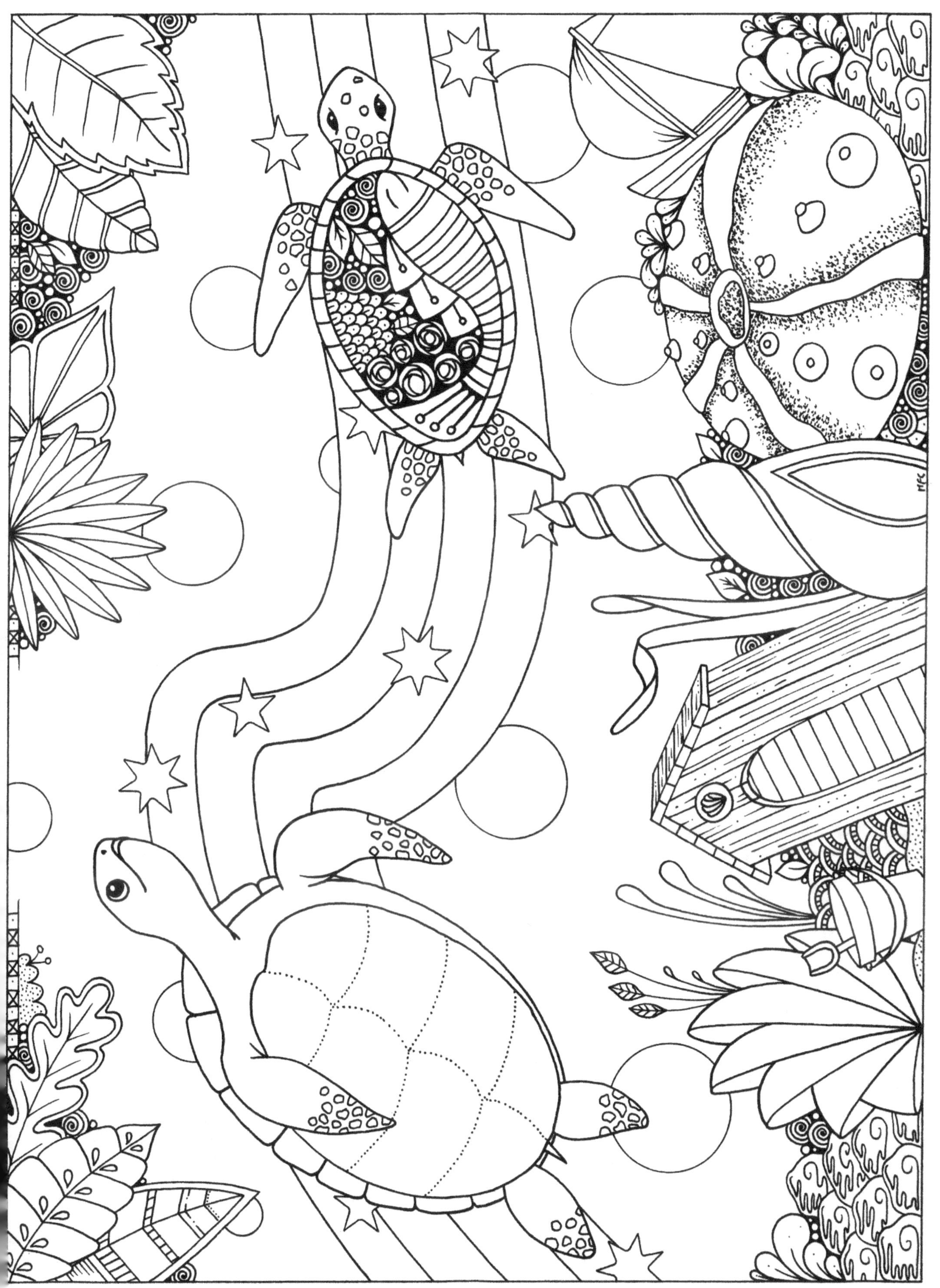

Maud Feral-Chauveau (MFC)

Back to the sea

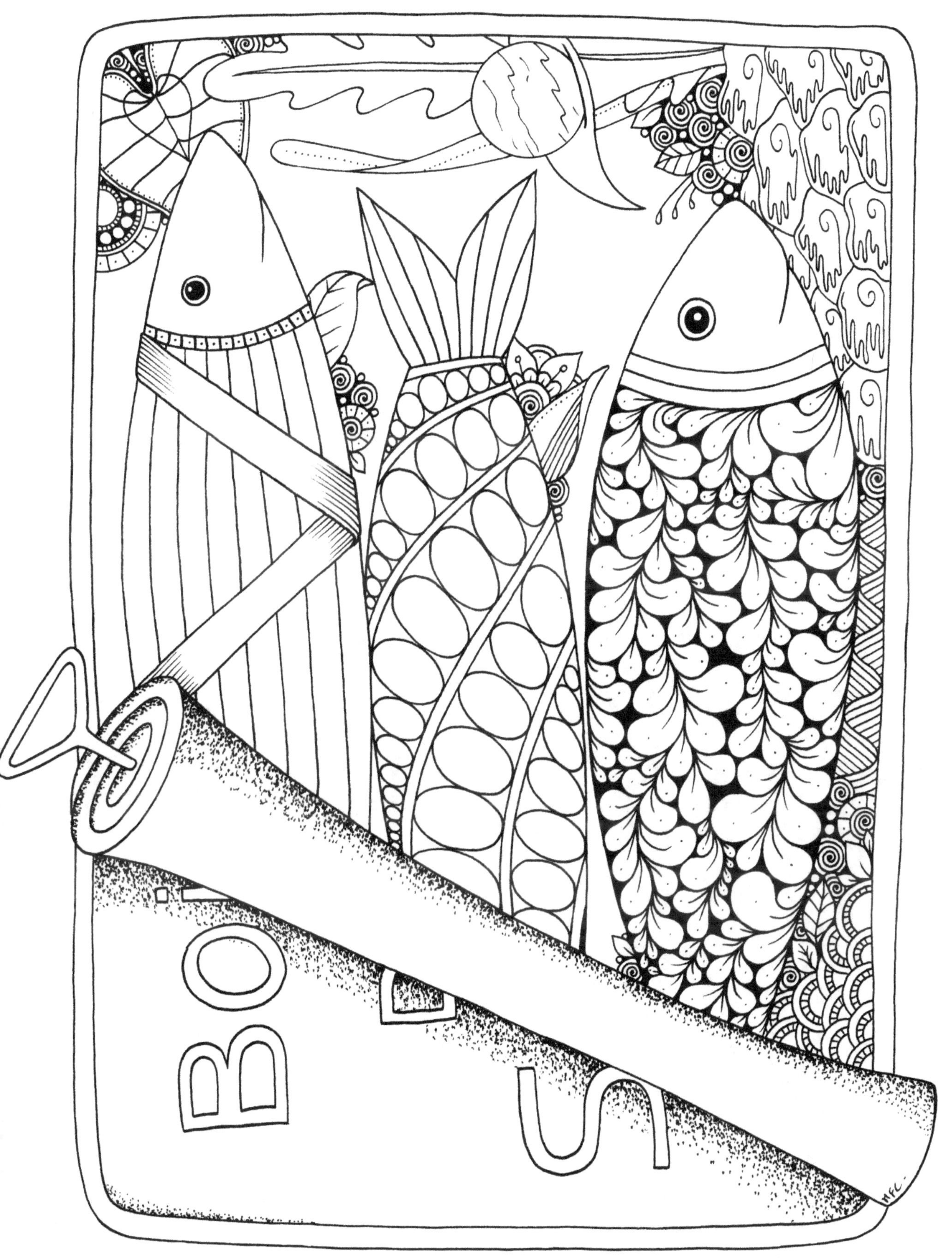

BO
JE
US

Maud Feral-Chauveau (MFC)

Back to the sea

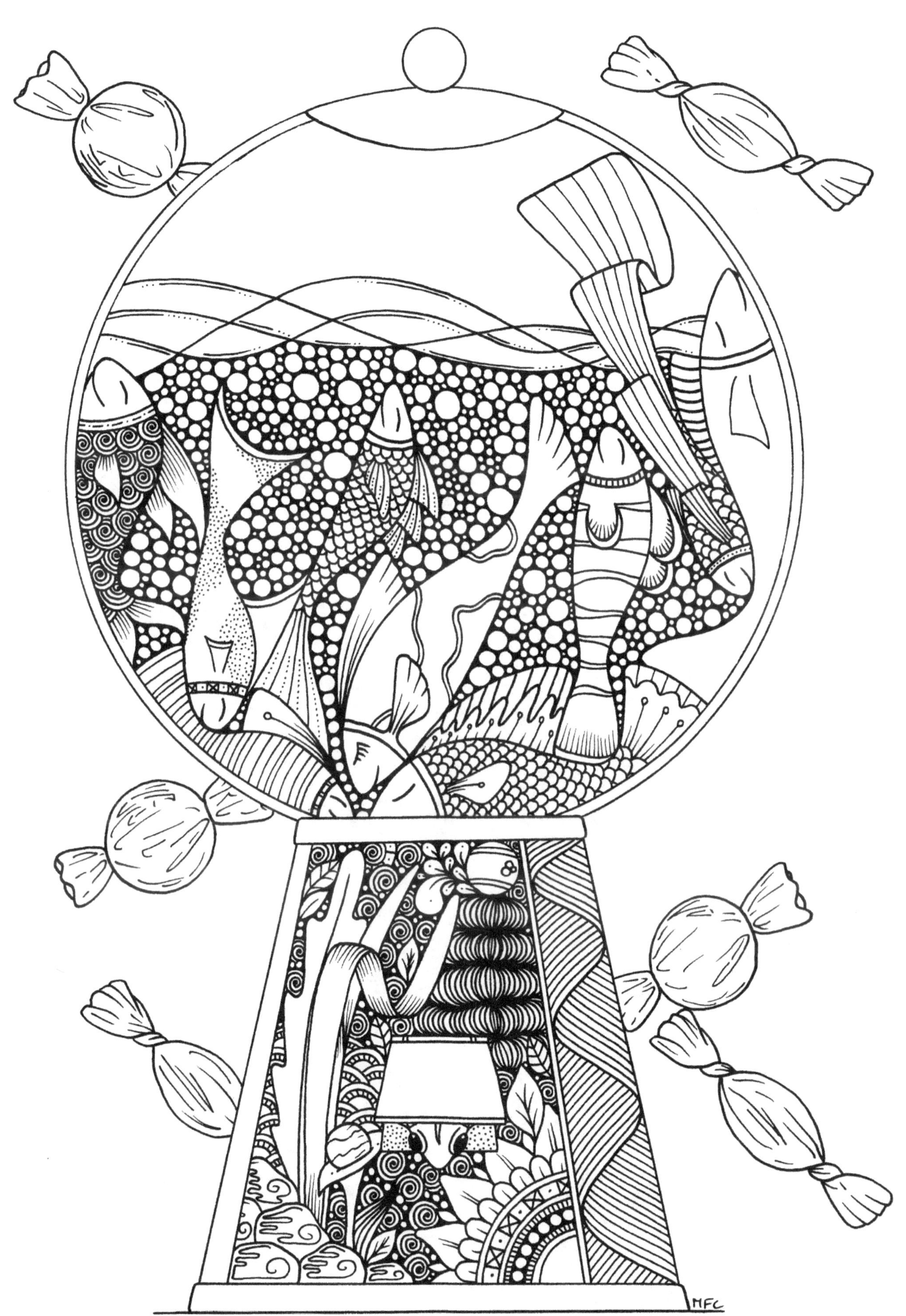

Maud Feral-Chauveau (MFC)

Back to the sea

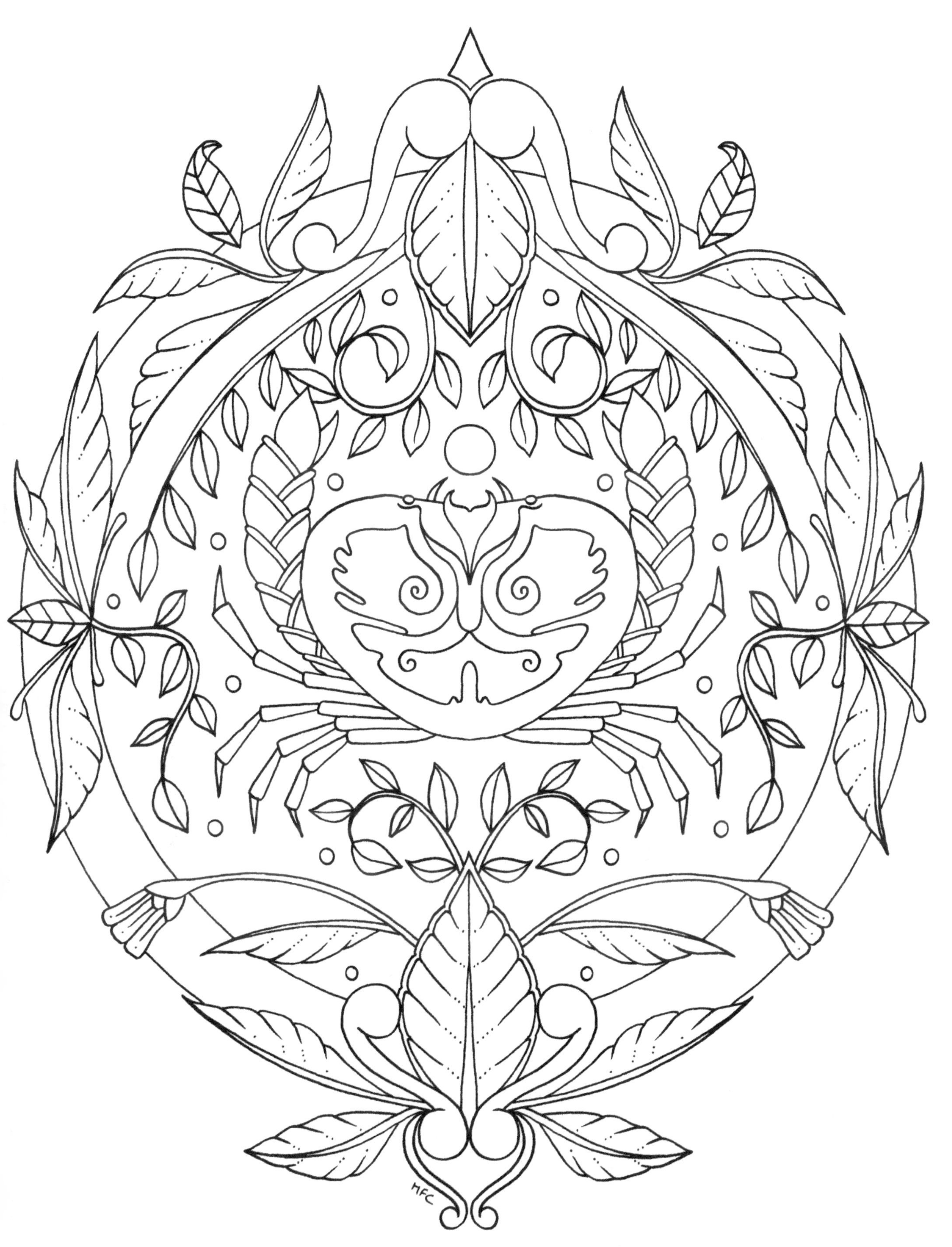

Maud Feral-Chauveau (MFC)

Back to the sea

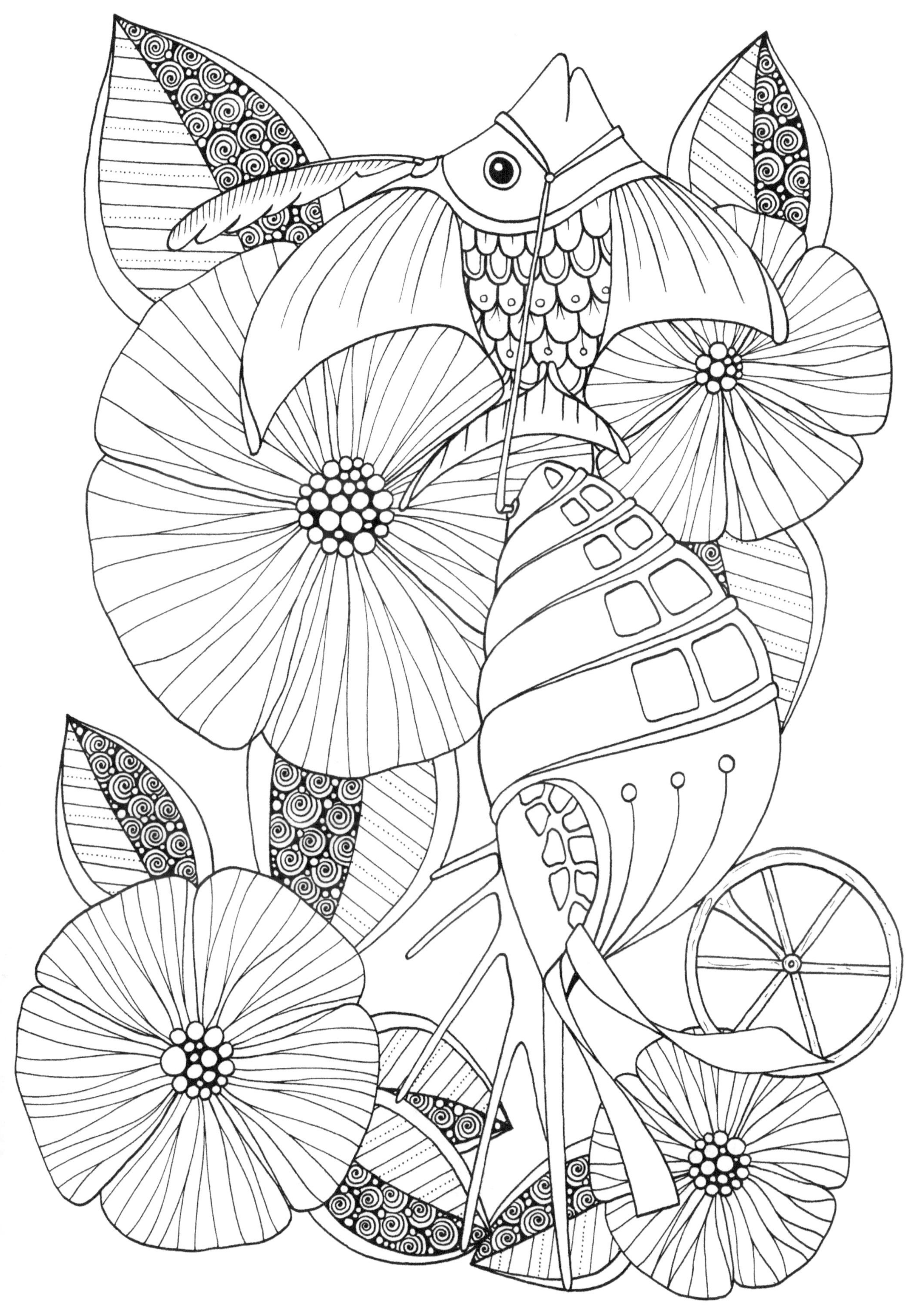

Maud Feral-Chauveau (MFC)

Back to the sea

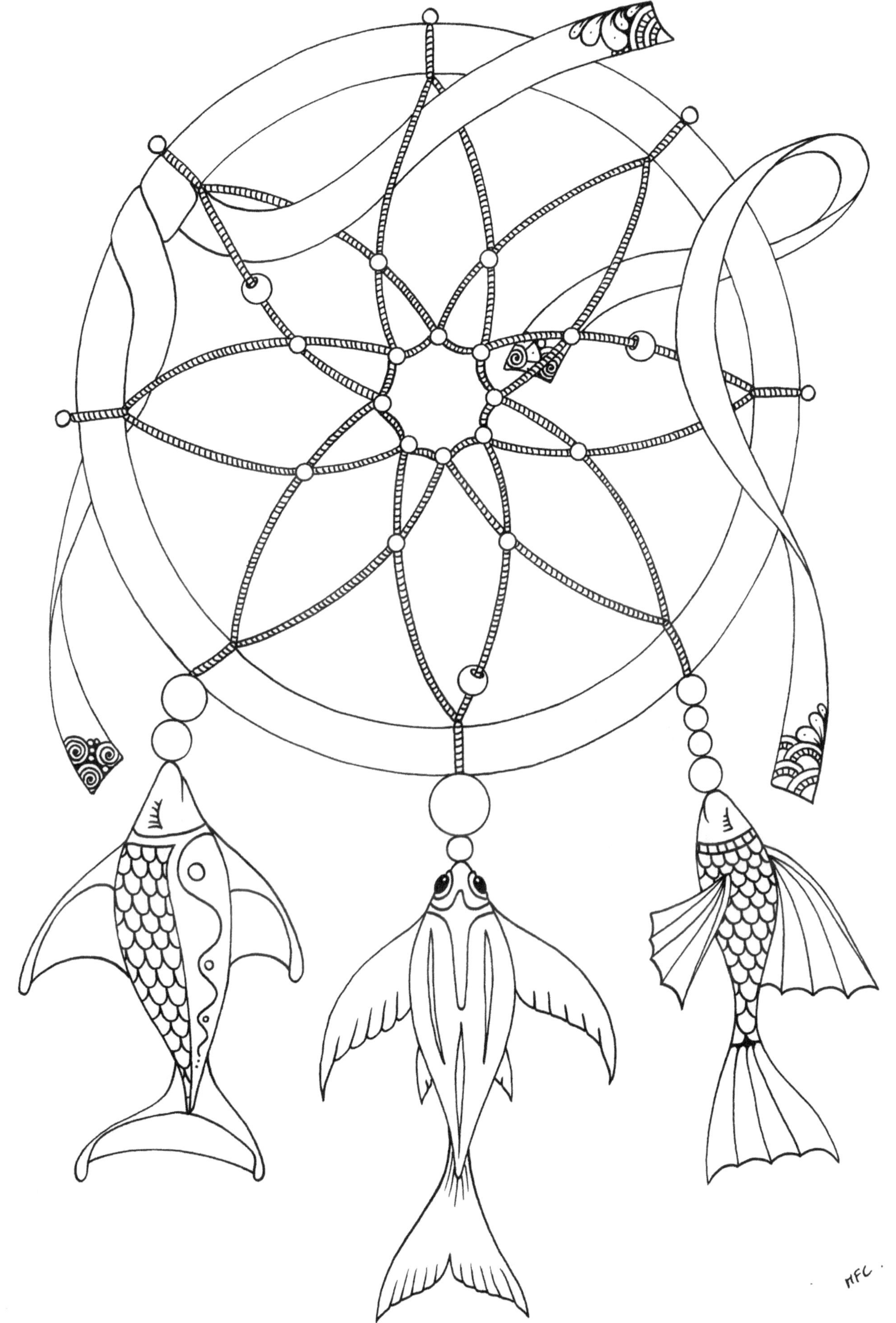

Maud Feral-Chauveau (MFC)

Back to the sea

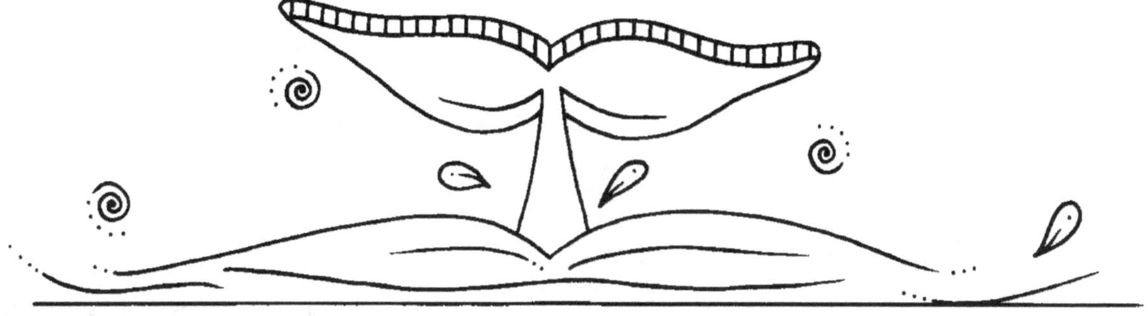

*I will be really happy to see your colors and to share with you,
also join me on my Facebook page.
See you soon*

*https://www.facebook.com/MFC-Peinture-graphisme-
illustrations*

*Other books by the same author (availbale on Amazon)
- The feet in the water
- A pencil on the heart
- Color your Kimmidoll*

*Je serais ravie de voir vos mises en couleurs et de partager avec vous
dans la convivialité,
alors rejoignez moi sur ma page Facebook.
À bientôt*

9791091517171

www.ingramcontent.com/pod-product-compliance
Lightning Source LLC
Chambersburg PA
CBHW080003180726
48002CB00020B/2938